OPPORTUNITIES IN
COMPUTER
MAINTENANCE
CAREERS

Elliott S. Kanter

Foreword by
Jonathan Yaeger
President & CEO
Atlanta Technical Specialists, Inc.

 **VGM Career Horizons**
a division of *NTC Publishing Group*
Lincolnwood, Illinois USA

Library of Congress Cataloging–in–Publication Data

Kanter, Elliott S.
    Opportunities in computer maintenance careers / Elliott S. Kanter
; foreword by Jonathan Yaeger.
        p.   cm. — (VGM opportunities series)
    Includes bibliographical references.
    ISBN 0–8442–4444–9 (h). — ISBN 0–8442–4445–7 (s)
    1. Computers—Maintenance and repair—Vocational guidance.
I. Title. II. Series.
TK7887.K36   1995
621.39′028′8—dc20   94–49351
                                                         CIP

1996 Printing

Published by VGM Career Horizons, a division of NTC Publishing Group.
© 1995 by NTC Publishing Group
4255 West Touhy Avenue
Lincolnwood (Chicago), Illinois 60646-1975 U.S.A. All rights reserved.

6 7 8 9 0 VP 9 8 7 6 5 4 3 2

CONTENTS

ABOUT THE AUTHOR

Elliott S. Kanter is a full-time technical writer specializing in the application and exploitation of high technology. Currently the owner and operator of a technical writing service, Technical Communications, located in Smyrna, Georgia, he writes for a number of high-technology and computer-related companies and is a frequent contributor to electronics and computer magazines. He is the author of *Servicing Biomedical Equipment* and *Servicing Electrocardiographs,* two pioneer practical guides for biomedical equipment technologists, and is known as a speaker and author in the areas of marketing and promoting high technology.

He received his bachelor's degree from Mundelein College in Chicago. He is a member of the Society for Technical Communications and a past member of the American Society of Medical Writers, AAMI, and the American Society of Hospital Engineers.

ACKNOWLEDGMENTS

The author wishes to thank the following individuals, companies, and agencies without whose help and cooperation this book could not have been written: Mr. George Keller, executive vice president, Association of Field Service Managers; the Computer and Business Equipment Manufacturers Association (CBEMA); Mr. Dwight Johnson, Abbott Medical Electronics; Intermedics Corp.; IBM; Cleveland Institute of Electronics (CIE); Heald Institute of Technology; Mr. Jonathan Yaeger, president and CEO, Atlanta Technical Specialists, Inc.; National Radio Institute (NRI); National Technical School (NTS); Mr. Bill Stewart; Heath Co.; Ms. Peggy Flanagan, U.S. Army Recruiting Command, Ft. Sheridan, Illinois; the officers and enlisted personnel of the U.S. Army's Computer Maintenance School, Fort Gordon, Georgia; the U.S. Department of Labor; SFC John C. Judd, Station Commander, U.S. Army Recruiting Station, Savannah, Georgia; the U.S. Air Force Training Command; and especially Lt. Green, the U.S. Navy Recruiting Service; Harris/3M Customer Service; Trend Tec; Mr. John Shadwick, manager, Field Engineering/Service; Toshiba U.S.A.; and all of the many individuals and companies who have contributed privately and anonymously to making this a useful and practical career guide.

The author also graciously acknowledges the editorial assistance of Ellen Urban.

FOREWORD

Popular careers come and go, but it is hard to think of a field that is more viable or promising than computer maintenance.

The microcomputer chip is ubiquitous. Wristwatches, cars, coffee-makers, and VCRs use them. As they proliferate, they become cheaper and more powerful. And as their number increases, so do career opportunities, especially in service and repair.

Some microcomputer devices are essentially "disposable." The personal computer is almost a commodity; someday replacement may cost less than repair. However, there will always be maintenance opportunities as long as businesses depend upon them. Hard drives crash, monitors grow dim, printers wear out, and someone must fix them.

The computer maintenance field is a service industry; it has become very *service oriented.* Successful service specialists must possess good people skills, be adept at communication, think clearly and logically, and be detail oriented. The best in the field have the same attributes as other successful people: they combine a broad range of knowledge with lots of hands-on experience, and they love what they do. Many have taken up electronics as a hobby, but there are no prerequisites (for example, I majored in English in college, but my specialty is component-level repair, or finding one bad part out of dozens or hundreds in a PC).

Increasingly, knowledge of software is an important part of the maintenance process. There is so much information on new hardware and software, that it is impossible to know all of the latest developments. Although that is part of the challenge, it is also part of the great excitement.

Compensation varies with the level of expertise. Entry-level salaries start at about $18,000 per year. Experienced specialists (especially those with network or other software knowledge) can earn as much as $50,000 per year. Good people are hard to come by and remain in high demand.

Opportunities in Computer Maintenance Careers provides an insightful and informative introduction and overview of the field. No doubt it will be a helpful and valuable reference for career planning in an industry with a bright and vast horizon.

Jonathan Yaeger
President & CEO
Atlanta Technical Specialists, Inc.

PREFACE

It may have happened already, or it might happen as you are reading these words, but one thing's for certain; within a relatively short period of time, the 100 millionth personal computer will be or has been sold!

Think about it. That number is about four times the total population of the state of California, and applies *only* to personal computers, not the mid-range or large systems that are still being built and used by industry and government.

When the first edition of this book went to print, the sales of personal computers was about 25 million over some four years. Yet today, companies such as Compaq report sales in excess of 1.5 million computers each quarter. In fact, there are *more* personal computers in use today in home-based businesses than were sold during those same four years. Prices for computers have plummeted. When we first wrote this book, it was written on a state-of-the-art computer that cost some $2,600. It had a 30 mB hard drive, monochrome monitor, less than 2 mB of memory, and used a 80286 microprocessor. This computer was the top of the line, and best available then—but this is now, and that system would best qualify as a "boat-anchor." It is totally outdated and useful only for the most basic tasks. That same $2,600 today would buy the very latest in microcomputers with high resolution color display, at least a 300 mB hard drive, 8 mB of memory, a CD-ROM drive and sound card, and more accessories than were ever envisioned just a few short years ago!

No matter how you measure it, someone must build these computers, and of course someone must be available to repair and maintain them when something goes wrong. That someone could very well be you.

With the growth in sheer numbers of computers, we've found a different perception of what service is all about. The personal computer has invaded all aspects of our lives and materially changed how and where we work. Because of these changes, our dependence upon that device on our desk has increased to the point that a failure or problem with the computer can and usually does materially affect the way we or our business or our school functions.

In the early days, if a computer failed, we accepted the fact that we'd probably have to crate it up and ship it back to the manufacturer, or at least physically carry it to the dealer or store where we purchased it. Today, with nearly 100 million of these systems in use, we aren't as understanding, and the norm is on-site service. A repair specialist comes to us! We don't carry the computer to them. They are dispatched to our home, school, or office and usually within a day. This service is taken for granted and included in a manufacturer's warranty and made part and parcel of service agreements—not just for businesses but for the system you may have in your home.

The line has blurred somewhat between servicing the hardware aspects of computers (the chips and other component parts that make up a computer) and the software-related activities that make a computer productive. Many times these problems are interwoven, and it takes a special sort of person to determine what component of a problem is hardware related, what part of the problem is software related, and then resolve both problems quickly and efficiently. One major equipment manufacturer has included a remote diagnostics program with all of the systems it sells. If you have a problem, a technician located many miles away can actually access your computer and run tests—all over your telephone line. Again, someone has to be there to run these tests, and that someone can be you!

Obviously, there have been some changes in the field of computer maintenance, and it is no longer enough to be technically competent. There are so many computers in the hands of so many different people that a high degree of communications skills are as important as your technical ability. You have to be able to deal with people—all kinds of people. Some will be technically adept and competent, others will be totally lacking in any understanding of the computer other than the fact that it doesn't work or isn't doing what they think it should. After all, anyone with about $1,200 can buy more raw computer power than most of this country's largest corporations had at their disposal just a few short years ago. Some things don't change. The more you learn, the more you'll earn, and with advances in computer technology coming at virtually the speed of light, you need all the education you can get, not just in technical areas but in communications skills as well. You'll be the human interface between this awesome computer power and the end user, and frequently, that user will not even know how to turn the computer on.

DEDICATION

In memory of my father, to whom education was one of life's greatest joys.

CHAPTER 1

GROWTH AND DIVERSITY OF THE FIELD

Don't take my word for it, most careers you might consider have roots, a history, a past that covers hundreds of years. The techniques might be different today, but essentially we make shoes and clothes much the same way they were made in the 1800s, and the same could be said about a great many of the ways people make their livings. Accountants still add and subtract numbers, dentists pull and fill teeth, and you could probably add dozens of examples of how little things really change in certain career fields. We could say that most, if not all, career fields available to you today are essentially the same as those that were available to your parents, their parents, and their parents' parents.

On the other hand, this book isn't about most careers, it's about a career in computer maintenance, and believe me, there isn't much about this career that could be considered history *unless* you consider something that happened in the last fifty or so years of historical significance. A time line depicting the history of computers wouldn't stretch very far. In fact, depending upon who you ask and how you qualify your question, the computer has just barely celebrated a half-century of existence. The personal computer, of which there are probably now some 100 million, first debuted in the 1980s, so our time line wouldn't stretch very far in comparison with other career fields.

Perhaps no other field has seen the dynamic growth that seems commonplace in the computer industry. Applications for computers and the computers themselves seem to proliferate as quickly as the speed of these computers increases. Entire industries and even words added to our vocabulary mimic the growth of what many have said will be the next industrial revolution, except instead of the *industrial age,* we will be in the *information age.* The physical size of the computer has shrunk from a room full of complex, heat-generating vacuum tubes to a small, handheld, personal data assistant powered by penlight batteries.

The average consumer today can command more computing power for less than $2,000 than the giants of industry had at their disposal just ten short years ago. And this computer is easier to use, costs less, and virtually anyone can exploit its advantages and join the information age. Considering that there are more personal computers being used for home-based businesses than there are people in the state of California, it's no wonder that this is the growth career field not for the next five, ten, or twenty years, but probably for the next century.

Few if any of the products we take for granted would be possible without the computer: your car's carburetor has given way to computer-controlled fuel injection, and the windup watch on your wrist is now quartz controlled, accurate to a second a month, digital and disposable. Life as we knew it before the computer will never be the same.

A BRIEF HISTORY OF TIME

Though it is not our intention to turn this book into a history of computers, it would be to our advantage to look back a few years at how our modern high-technology devices evolved. This will be a short trip back into time, focusing on the computer or high-technology device as we understand it today rather than examining its historical past in the traditional sense. What might qualify as ancient history to this field could be defined as something that happened some fifty years ago, when computers and computing devices were mechanical rather than electronic.

Just a few decades ago, these computers and calculators were so large they occupied rooms of their own. One such machine was the very large and cumbersome automatic sequence controller calculator produced by IBM (International Business Machines Corporation). The device was very large and, by today's standards, quite slow. It was designed to automate accounting procedures and was essentially a giant, cumbersome calculator. But it was a computer or computing device. Its size was a direct result of the technology in effect fewer than forty years ago. Fragile glass electronic components called vacuum tubes, which required vast amounts of electrical power, produced equally large amounts of heat and took up space, thus making this device as difficult and costly to keep cool as it was to store. Yet only a few decades later, all of the functions and capabilities of this early computer—and then some—could be had in a portable, battery-operated laptop computer. We can readily see what a difference thirty very short years can make.

As the 1940s were drawing to a close, scientists at Bell Laboratories made a fascinating discovery, one that would forever change the course and direction of high technology. This discovery was the transistor. Transistors, unlike vacuum tubes, were small, didn't produce much heat, could operate from batteries or low-voltage supplies, and most of all, would allow engineers to develop smaller and faster devices that could be mass produced. The humble laboratory experiments led to the pocket-sized transistor radio, and the technology moved forward. The term *solid-state device* became a part of our vocabulary and came to be used to refer to anything from simple radios to complex electronic devices. But this was only the beginning.

Technology was on the move, and within about a dozen years came the integrated circuit. A close cousin to the transistor, the integrated circuit, or ic, relied upon a sophisticated combination of chemistry and photography to reproduce complex circuits and components on silicon wafer chips. These chips, some fifty or more to a silicon wafer about an inch in diameter, could contain hundreds of electronic components, each matched for specific characteristics and functions. Like the transistor, the ic's power requirements were modest and its size very small. High technology was really on its way. Entire blocks of circuitry formerly requiring vast amounts of space, using vacuum-tube technologies or even transistors, were reduced onto chips measuring less than a square inch.

As technology advanced, so did the integrated circuit. Such terms as LSI (large-scale integration), where a single chip contained more than a thousand components, gave way to VLSI (very large-scale integration), where the small chip could contain all the components required to make a complete computing device. For example, the actual size of a computer-controlled pacemaker, a device usually placed inside the body to regulate a faulty heart, is smaller than a dime. The size of the chip gives you some idea of the complexity possible using today's technology and how small an ic has become.

Our history lesson is rapidly coming to a close. In a few paragraphs we've examined some of the developments that make today's career opportunities in computer maintenance what they are and have indicated how rapidly things have evolved. There are very few areas of our lives still untouched or as yet uninfluenced by a computer. If you don't believe this, stop for a moment and think about the things around you and that you use every day. For example, the digital watch on your wrist is a form of computer. The keypad on a microwave oven is used to tell a microcomputer or microprocessor how long to cook and at what temperature. The carburetor on cars has been replaced by microprocessor-controlled electronic fuel injection, and many banking transactions take place at teller machines, which serve as stand-alone links to a main bank's computer system. All of these changes have occurred in less than fifty years. In fact, most have taken place in the last dozen or so years, as technology has brought the cost of computing power down to the point both financially and in physical size to allow computers—formerly reserved for large corporations—to find their way into small businesses, schools, and even homes. The high-technology field is waiting for you and changing at the same time. Today's science fiction may be tomorrow's reality.

THE PROLIFIC AND EVER-PRESENT COMPUTER

The manuscript for this book was written on a computer. So perhaps it is fitting to explore one of the most common uses of computers today: word processing. Word processing combines the computer and a specifically designed software program to produce letter-perfect text. Unlike the common typewriter, the computer first displays the words you type on a screen called a CRT (cathode-ray tube), then temporarily stores them in RAM (random-access memory) integrated circuits, and finally provides a permanent storage facility in the form of either a floppy diskette or on a fixed disk drive. The completed text can then be sent to a printer to produce the finished typed page (hard copy).

This compares to a great extent to the process of typing a letter on a conventional typewriter. However, the typewriter offers some temporary advantages. The text appears letter-by-letter on the paper page with no steps in between. Though at first it would seem that the computer is being wasted and turned into a large and expensive electronic typewriter, the software, or word-processing program, offers many advantages to anyone who produces information. Text may be moved about, changed, or reformatted to a specific requirement on a computer. Errors, especially spelling errors, are checked and corrected before the text or information is committed to a final hard-copy printout. Corrections, changes, or additions do not require the entire document to be retyped. It's as easy to move an entire paragraph as it is to move a word. All of the repetitious actions present on a typewriter are not present with the computer. Another bonus is speed. Using a typewriter, your skill in its operation, that is to say, how fast and accurately you type, will determine how long it takes to produce a letter. Using the computer, your typing speed becomes less of an issue. Regardless of how fast you type the individual letters, the computer and the printer can process and print out the information at typical speeds in excess of two hundred words per minute—far above even the most skilled typist. For this reason, a major application for at least the desktop computer is the preparation and processing of words and information. But like most applications we have discussed, the technology is recent. The dependency of a business on its computer system has become great.

Computers are also used to manipulate data. The manipulation of data, or number-crunching, as it is widely called, represents the most common application of a computer in business. Computers are best at manipulating numbers or data. They are fast and accurate, and they can perform the same tasks over and over again without tiring or making errors. For example, certain software programs known as spreadsheet programs allow a business to answer the question "What if?" by changing figures into graphics and viewing the results almost immediately.

Not all computers are visible or even resemble the typical PC. Take for instance the complete microprocessor-controlled pacemaker, ready to be placed within the chest of a patient whose heart is not capable of regulating its activities alone. Medicine and medical devices use computers extensively to collect and manipulate information and to directly control or change how parts of the body work.

The field of biomedical engineering, medicine combined with high-technology, is a fast-growing and very exciting career option for computer service specialists. Granted, you won't be asked to repair a pacemaker or similar device inside a patient, but you will have a unique opportunity to join hands with medical health care providers.

Computers, or microprocessors, are also found in other applications. Specially equipped computers even design other computers and complex devices. Computer-aided design and computer-aided manufacturing (CAD/CAM) rely upon the computer to replace or assist the human operator in preparing equipment designs, architectural drawings, blueprints, and even complex integrated circuit layouts to a degree and scale impossible for an operator to produce unassisted. The computer's ability to manipulate data and to translate the information to graphic representations covers a large segment of the use of computers today. However, the computer's involvement doesn't stop with design. It extends to the floor of a manufacturing facility in the form of process control and robotics.

Building any product requires labor. Labor costs are rising, causing many industries to turn away from traditional markets to underdeveloped countries and other sources of inexpensive labor. In order for any manufacturing to exist or continue to compete in today's market, costs must be contained, and computer technology offers just that competitive edge. Process controllers do exactly what the name implies. They control or direct a specific process. For example, assume that a metal plate requires holes to be drilled every three inches. A drill-press operator could stand at a machine for eight hours a day drilling these holes, or a form of computer-controlled drilling machine could do the job automatically. Such computer-controlled machines are usually referred to as N/C or numerically controlled devices. They mate the microprocessor for control with a drilling machine, and they rely on a tape or other program to allow for instructions to flow between the computer controller and the machine. An operator might merely insert the unfinished metal plate and remove the finished, drilled product.

Robotics, on the other hand, does away with the operator. Sophisticated combinations of electronics and mechanical devices work together to duplicate the operator's actions. Automobile assembly lines use robotic welding machines to make the hundreds of individual welds necessary to produce a car. These robotic devices are controlled by a computer system, follow specific instructions, and repeat the same task over and over again. The robot device may only be a moving arm attached to a tool, serviced by a computer, but it never tires, takes coffee breaks, or asks for a raise.

Manufacturing is a growing user of computers, both for traditional data manipulations and for assistance in the physical activities of making a product. As with the other fields we have explored, if there are computers, or computer-controlled devices, there must be a need for computer service specialists.

Computers are also a major part of a growth industry unheard of even a few short years ago. Although we find that labor costs have eroded our manufacturing base, a whole new field has opened to us, courtesy of the personal computer. Rather than simply building products, the future according to many experts is in supplying and manipulating information.

The much used phrase "The Information Highway" is an electronic ribbon that has literally linked most of the world via computers. A student or businessperson in New York is only a keystroke or two away from a counterpart in California, or for that matter Istanbul. Vast repositories of information located hundreds or thousands of miles away are as near as your computer and keyboard. Satellites and telephone lines link most of the world as we know it, and information passes through these links at speeds unheard of even two years ago.

During the Desert Storm Campaign, our tanks operating in the barren desert were able to pinpoint their positions within about a square meter using tiny computers that were linked to satellites flying in outer space. Ships at sea, or airplanes, or for that matter campers can determine exactly where they are using the same technology.

We are progressing from the industrial age to the information age, where many of the jobs created will be the result of processing information. No device is better at manipulating information than the computer, especially now that the personal computer has achieved the speed and sheer processing power of yesterday's mammoth systems and products such as graphic interfaces (Windows, Macintosh) have made exploiting this power almost gamelike.

Again, this new industry is totally dependent upon the computer, and if the computer fails, then the wheels of industry come to an abrupt stop! Someone, somewhere has to be able to jump-start this stalled computer, and the field of computer maintenance is one that can only grow and expand just the same way these computers proliferate. And this growth is not only in our country—it's global in scope. Eastern Europe, emerging from decades of communism, is a major consumer of technology. They will be buying systems, and someone will have to install and maintain their new base of technology.

As the preceding few examples illustrate, computers or high-technology devices have, in a relatively short period, come to greatly touch and affect our lives. And the technology that enables their development is continuing to grow at a terrific pace. Consequently, no other occupational field offers such unlimited opportunities or challenges—or diversity—as high technology. This book will explore the entire field of opportunities in computer maintenance careers.

CHAPTER 2

EDUCATIONAL REQUIREMENTS

In this chapter we will explore educational requirements for a career in computer maintenance, how these requirements can be met, and how we learn. By the time you opened this book, in many ways you were already quite an expert on how you learn and perhaps even why you don't learn. You have spent at least ten years furthering your education and are preparing to spend anywhere from a year to four years more preparing for a career after you've finished high school.

TRADITIONAL AND NONTRADITIONAL
METHODS OF LEARNING

Have you ever given much thought to how you learn something? How you learn is nearly as important as what you learn. There are traditional and nontraditional ways of learning. You are probably more familiar with what is called the traditional method. You attend school, sit in classes, and a teacher imparts information to you and your classmates. This information can be in the form of lectures, assigned readings from textbooks, or information you collectively arrive at by means of experimentation. Traditional education is highly structured and disciplined. There are set goals and some forms of validating or testing to ensure that knowledge has been transferred from the teacher to the student.

Nontraditional education, on the other hand, is somewhat less structured and more free-flowing. Knowledge is transferred from one source to another in much the same manner found in a classroom, but the techniques are quite different. Think back a few years to the time you learned to ride a bike. There was no textbook to teach you how and there was no classroom. But there was a teacher, though perhaps not in the school-student sense. This time the teacher could have been a parent, brother, or sister. You learned by following instructions, observing an example, and by doing. This was a nontraditional method of instruction and learning in its simplest form, a sort of on-the-job education.

We learn by combinations of traditional and nontraditional methods. Some things are best learned in the structure of traditional education, but other things can be learned just as well by nontraditional methods. For years the military taught skills to soldiers and sailors using nontraditional on-the-job training. You may even have relatives who started their careers as apprentices who participated in long-term on-the-job training in a construction trade. Many years ago even doctors and lawyers learned their respective professions by serving an apprenticeship and learning by doing from someone already skilled in their field. You may even have relatives or friends who have taken home-study or correspondence courses. All of these are examples of nontraditional forms of education. In this book we will explore both the conventional or traditional way of preparing for a career in computer maintenance and also the unique opportunities for nontraditional educational preparation available today.

CBEMA GUIDELINES

The Computer and Business Equipment Manufacturers Association (CBEMA) published a booklet in 1981 called *Educational Guidelines for Service Technicians.* According to this book, prepared by members of the industry you are preparing to enter, the guidelines are divided into the following categories:

- Personal skills
- Interpersonal relations and communications

- Mathematics—basic mathematics, units of measure, computers
- Basic mechanics—fastening devices, pins and keys, soldering, mechanical drawings, safety
- Electronics—basic electronics, electrical symbols and diagrams, logic circuitry, block and timing diagrams
- Tools and test equipment—hand tools and power tools, electronic test equipment
- Parts handling
- Report and record-keeping administration—reports, map reading

Each of these categories has a corresponding list of objectives that must be met in order to satisfy the overall requirements as determined by the industry. Let's examine these requirements in detail. You might be surprised at what skills you already have, and of course, you will have the opportunity to view some of the skill areas you will need to master.

Personal Skills

This guideline covers students' personal abilities and traits. The students should demonstrate the ability to do the following:

- Repair a piece of equipment or an assembly that requires them to work in a physically awkward or difficult position according to the same standards they would achieve in an ideal location.
- Repair cheerfully and successfully a piece of inoperative equipment when the customer is very disturbed or angry.
- Complete a series of tasks requiring them to work alone for eight hours, just as they would under the direction of a supervisor.
- Accurately follow each and every step in a long adjustment procedure.

Interpersonal Relations and Communications

Students should demonstrate the ability to do the following:

- Use clear, concise, and technically accurate language to explain to a co-worker how to make a particular mechanical, electrical, or

pneumatic adjustment so that the co-worker can make the adjustment correctly.
- Answer a salesperson's question about equipment operation accurately, clearly, and in a positive manner.
- Present effectively to supervisors their positions in conflicts with customers, co-workers, or salespeople.
- Prepare clearly, concisely, and accurately a job application and a résumé.

Mathematics

This category is broken down into three parts: basic mathematics, units of measure, and computers.

BASIC MATHEMATICS

Students must be able to do the following:

- Add and subtract accurately.
- Multiply and divide accurately.
- Calculate powers of ten.

UNITS OF MEASURE

Students must be able to do the following:

- Measure with a common rule (English or metric to the tolerance of the scale in use).
- Convert, making no errors, fractions to decimals and decimals to fractions.

COMPUTERS

Students must be able to add and subtract correctly in the following numeration systems:
- Binary
- Octal
- Hexadecimal

The student must be able to convert numbers from one base to another without error.

Basic Mechanics

Students must be able to do the following:

- Understand how levers, gears, chains, sprockets, belts, and pulleys are used to increase or decrease the mechanical advantage and speed of motion.
- Adjust solenoids for proper operation.
- Adjust microswitches for proper over-travel and release.
- Adjust tension properly on belt and chain drives, with and without idlers.
- List the proper lubrication of the following parts under all operating conditions:
  1. Gearboxes
  2. Oilite bearings on shafts
  3. Plastic bearings on metal shafts
  4. Plastic to plastic
  5. Metal to metal
- Identify defective parts among the following, describing the cause and result of their condition:
  1. Relay contacts
  2. Motor brushes
  3. Motor commutators
  4. Pins (sockets in connectors)
  5. Broken wires (hidden by insulation)
  6. Frayed wires
  7. Frozen bearings
  8. Stretched chains
  9. Bent levers
  10. Bushings
  11. Scored shafts
  12. Bent shafts
  13. Out-of-round shafts
  14. Gears
  15. Broken teeth on gears
  16. Sprockets
  17. Deformed springs
  18. Pulleys

FASTENING DEVICES

Students must be able to identify and provide examples of the use of the following types of screws and fasteners:

1. Machine
2. Sheet metal
3. Fine thread
4. Coarse thread
5. Self-tapping
6. Setscrews
7. Capscrews
8. Hex head
9. Allen head
10. Flat head
11. Thumbscrew
12. Fillister head
13. Phillips head

PINS AND KEYS

Identify and provide examples of the use of the following pins:

1. Spiral
2. Dowel
3. Tapered
4. Roll
5. Cotter

Remove each of the following types of pins and keys so that it may be used again:

Pins	Keys
Spiral	Square
Dowel	Woodruff
Tapered	
Roll	
Cotter	

Remove and install each of the following types of rings:

1. Truarc (inside and outside)

2. E-Rings
3. O-Rings

Remove and install the following types of nuts, giving reasons for their use:

1. Hex
2. Jam
3. Castellated
4. Wing
5. Cap
6. Thumb
7. Stop
8. Tinnerman

Be able to list the problems that would result from stripped and cross-threaded screws and nuts.

SOLDERING

Students should demonstrate the ability to do the following:

- Remove and replace an integrated circuit (ic) on a printed circuit board using the following equipment:
  1. Vacuum and desoldering tool
  2. Solder braid
  3. Heat sinks
  4. Flux cleaner
  5. Soldering irons (various wattage)
  6. Fluxes
  7. Solder
  8. Tip cleaning equipment
- Demonstrate their soldering technique so that the following are achieved:
  1. The foil on the circuit board is intact.
  2. The ic tests properly, and the circuit board does not show any burn spots or cold-solder joints.
  3. Remove and replace soldered wire connectors to plugs and circuit boards.
  4. Make in-line soldered splices to wire cable harnesses.

MECHANICAL DRAWINGS

Students will demonstrate the ability to do the following:

- Describe the function of a mechanical device pictured in a cutaway drawing.

SAFETY

Students will demonstrate the ability to do the following:

- Use properly functioning tools and test equipment in a safe and effective manner.
- Use the proper technique for lifting and moving heavy equipment.
- Demonstrate CPR (cardiopulmonary resuscitation).

Electronics

This category is divided into four parts: basic electronics, electrical symbols and diagrams, logic circuitry, and block and timing diagrams.

BASIC ELECTRONICS

Students will demonstrate the ability to do the following:

1. Solve simple electrical circuits using Ohm's law.
2. Solve for resistance, voltage, currents, and wattages in series, parallel, and series-parallel circuits using Ohm's law.
3. Measure currents and voltages in AC circuits containing resistance, inductance, and capacitance.
4. Define common-base, common-emitter, and common-collector transistor circuit characteristics.

ELECTRICAL SYMBOLS AND DIAGRAMS

Students will demonstrate the ability to match a specific point on a schematic representation of an electronic circuit to its part on the electronic component:

1. Anode of a diode
2. Base, collector, and emitter of a transistor
3. Gate of a triac
4. Specific pin (that is, pin 8) of an ic

5. Clear or reset input to a microprocessor
- Follow a signal from start to finish on schematic representation of more than two different circuit boards.
- Determine points where signal flow can be checked on the circuit boards.
- Describe the condition and purpose of each of the following active devices on a schematic representation with signal inputs:

Diodes	Triacs
Transistors	Zener diodes
LEDs	Relays
SCRs	Microswitches

LOGIC CIRCUITRY

Students should demonstrate the ability to do the following:

- Wire and verify the input and output circuitry of logic gates using truth tables.

BLOCK AND TIMING DIAGRAMS

Students should demonstrate the ability to do the following:

- Define the uses of electrical and mechanical block diagrams and the function and use of timing diagrams.

Tools and Test Equipment

Students will demonstrate the ability to select and use the following tools to complete a series of mechanical tasks:

HAND TOOLS AND POWER TOOLS

Demonstrate tightening using the following:

1. Box and open-end wrenches
2. Hex wrenches
3. Ratchet-drive socket wrenches
4. Slip-joint pliers
5. Needlenose pliers
6. Screwdrivers

Demonstrate cutting using the following:

1. Hacksaw
2. Files and file card
3. Wire cutters
4. Wire strippers
5. Abrasive cloths

Demonstrate drilling using hand and power drills.

Demonstrate correct measuring techniques using the following:

1. Dial indicators
2. Thermometers (temperature gauges)
3. Feeler gauges

Perform soldering procedures using the following:

1. Soldering irons (various wattages)
2. Heat sinks
3. Solder braid
4. Desoldering tools
5. Tip-cleaning equipment

Demonstrate the use of the following other tools:

1. Center punches
2. O-ring removal tool
3. Hammers
4. Mirrors
5. Spring-hooking tools
6. Pin extractor

Demonstrate the proper use of electric grinder.

ELECTRONIC TEST EQUIPMENT

Students will demonstrate the ability to use the following test equipment to make specified measurements:

1. Oscilloscopes:
   a. Frequency
   b. Pulse width
   c. Amplitude
   d. Signal relationship

2. Volt-ohmmeters
3. Digital voltmeters
4. Ammeters

Parts Handling

Students will demonstrate the ability to arrange storage for the following parts so that each part can be easily located by means of a filing card system:

1. Shafts
2. Bearings (various types)
3. Circuit boards
4. Glass items
5. Lubricants
6. Small electronic parts
7. Hardware (assorted)
8. Rollers
9. Seals and gaskets
10. Plastic parts

Report and Record Keeping Administration

Students will demonstrate the ability to do the following:

- File (alphabetically or numerically) and rapidly retrieve an assortment of technical data.
- Add new data to or purge out-dated or redundant information from a well-organized file or collection of technical data.

REPORTS

Demonstrate the ability to do the following:

1. Complete an accurate time and activity report for a hypothetical work week.
2. Fill out an order form for parts needed, using a listing of parts used over the past year, a list of recommended parts to carry, and a list of parts on hand.
3. Accurately fill out service logs using correct technical terms.

MAP READING

Demonstrate the ability to find a given location on a map of the city. Indicate the best route to a given town on a state map marked with a starting point.

CBEMA's guidelines give both the job seeker and an educational institution an indication of what skill levels must be attained to enter the field of computer maintenance. You might have noticed that some of the skill requirements were familiar, while other terms were totally foreign. What is important at this point is that you have a clear understanding of what sorts of knowledge you will be expected to have in order to enter the field. With this bit of information covered, let's take a look at how you go about preparing to meet these requirements and the many options available to you. Some of the requirements can be met while you are still in high school, others can be learned on your own, or from books and kits. We will explore all of the ways you can prepare, and we will examine some actual course outlines from both traditional and nontraditional educational sources.

BUILDING A SOLID BASE

Considering all that you will have to learn and master, today, as you read this book, will be the best time to start preparing for a career in computer maintenance. Experts employed in the field stress the need for a firm foundation at the high school level before you begin to take on any further or specialized training. A good service specialist also will have excellent people skills. A well-rounded education provides the basis for getting along with others, so in addition to taking all of the science and mathematics courses available to you, you should take courses in literature, the social sciences, and the humanities. The more you can learn about people, cultures, and "what makes us what we are," the better you will find yourself prepared to take on a career where meeting and dealing with the public will either make or break you. If you are shy or hesitant about speaking to people, try a course in public speaking or drama. You won't become a professional actor, but you will develop poise and self-assurance when dealing with strangers or groups of people.

Some of the requirements set forth by CBEMA can be met with courses available to you right now. There are vocational and shop courses where you can learn how to handle tools safely and properly and where you can master basic electricity. Courses in drafting might also be available to help you get that competitive edge. Courses in creative writing or business communications can help you meet the requirements for report writing. If you have even the slightest idea that you'd like to own your own business, there are courses in bookkeeping, office procedures, business communications, and other related subjects that can meet your requirements for graduation and help you prepare for your career. Some experts recommend a foreign language, because much of the new technology is coming from sources outside the United States. Again, you won't be expected to be a linguist, but a basic knowledge of a foreign language can frequently be invaluable. Furthermore, don't overlook such extracurricular activities as the Computer Club, Junior Achievement, or service clubs. These organizations can provide additional skills and help you hone your ability to get along with others. Hobbies such as amateur radio can prepare you for some of the technical aspects of the field while widening your knowledge base.

Whatever you do, don't think about dropping out of school. There are no positions in the computer maintenance field for those without a minimum of a high school diploma. The old standby of enlisting in the military, getting a GED (general equivalence diploma), and then going into a high-tech field is now fiction! According to representatives from all branches of the military, they won't consider you for enlistment and training in any of the desirable fields without a high school diploma. One more word of advice, this from industry as well as the military: Don't get into trouble—no drinking, reckless driving, and no drugs! Anything other than a minor traffic infraction can cost you a career.

As a computer maintenance specialist, you may have to be able to obtain a security clearance in order to perform your job. Getting or not getting a security clearance can mean the difference between a job with a large company or the government or not getting a job at all. Security clearances attest to your reliability, stability, and loyalty. For jobs with the government, you are investigated and examined in-depth by federal officers who will review police and court records. As mentioned earlier, anything other than a routine traffic citation can disqualify you for a clearance, which in turn may limit your career growth. The U.S. Navy requires every computer maintenance specialist to be able to qualify for a "TOP SECRET" clearance before it will consider the individual for training. Certain Air Force, Army, and Marine occupational specialties carry similar restrictions,

AFTER HIGH SCHOOL

In the following chapters we will examine four methods of obtaining the training you'll need to enter the exciting field of computer maintenance after you've completed high school:

- Junior college/vocational technical schools
- Military training schools
- Home or correspondence schools
- Self-study

Two of these methods would qualify under the earlier definition of traditional education. These are the junior college/vocational technical school and the military. The remaining two, home or correspondence schools and self-study are definitely nontraditional forms of education that can and do satisfy the educational requirements for a career as a computer maintenance specialist. There is a bit of overlap within the military, where traditionally structured classroom instructional techniques are supplemented by extensive on-the-job training. Three of the four methods have in common that you will be responsible for the tuition and costs. The military, on the other hand, offers something unique. It will both train you and pay you while you learn. All of these alternatives are presented to assist you in making the best possible choice. A four-year college degree is not necessary for a career in computer maintenance.

CHAPTER 3

JUNIOR COLLEGE/VOCATIONAL TECHNICAL SCHOOL

WHAT DO THEY OFFER?

Junior colleges and vocational technical schools make up an important educational resource on a local level. The junior or community college can be either a state-supported institution or a privately owned institution. Likewise, vocational technical schools are run both by local and state governments and occasionally by private enterprises. Regardless of who runs the school, there will be strict guidelines for admission, and of course, there will be a number of fees including tuition, lab fees, and charges for books.

Junior or community colleges, as opposed to four-year colleges or universities, award associate degrees in specific career fields. They are most suitable for those entering fields such as computer maintenance where a four-year degree is not essential. Courses may be in either a degree or certificate program, with the degree programs requiring two years of school. Typically, these colleges offer an associate degree in electronics or computer technology to successful graduates.

Vocational technical schools can coexist within the framework of a junior or community college. Vocational technical schools frequently have special programs as their very reason for being. Vocational technical schools offer specialized programs that may or may not be available at the normal junior or community college. Typically, some of these special programs are of less than two years in length and have a certificate rather than an associate degree as the result for attendance and completion of requirements. Although this certificate program attests to abilities in a limited field, certificate holders do not fare well at an interview when the employer has a choice of hiring them or someone who has completed an associate degree program. For this reason, you are strongly advised to invest both your time and money in a program that will at least offer you an associate of science degree.

All colleges or vocational technical schools are not alike. It is important to ensure that the school you choose is accredited. This accreditation merely means that your state has examined the school and certifies that it meets minimum requirements to be an educational institution. You should beware of claims or phrases such as "Registered," "Approved for Veteran's Benefits" or any other statements that do not identify a state or federal agency as the source of the accreditation. Your education is both an investment in your future and an immediate cost to you or your parents for the tuition and fees. A smart shopper will investigate schools before signing any agreements. Regardless of how impressive the brochures or the list of accrediting agencies, it is in your best interest to do the following:

1. Visit the school. Meet administrators and instructors. Look at the students, facilities, and classrooms. Does it seem to meet your needs, or will you have to compromise your plans?
2. Try to talk to students. Are they satisfied with the training, facilities, and instructors?
3. Get names of graduates who have jobs and contact them. Ask them what kind of job they found, if their training prepared them for the job, and what salary are they earning.
4. Ask the administrator for the figures on students enrolled versus the number that graduate. How many of the students who started completed their education? How many of the students found jobs? What kinds of jobs did they find?

Take a long, hard look at the school's facilities. Entering a high-technology field requires up-to-date training as well as access to equipment for vital hands-on experience. Is there enough equipment in the labs to ensure that your time will be spent learning, not waiting your turn? Is there a well-equipped library? Does the school have a relationship with local industries? This relationship usually results in the school having access to equipment and guest lecturers from these companies, and this special relationship usually includes employment opportunities or preferential treatment for graduates with the participating firms.

COST OF EDUCATION

Tuition is based on a flat rate per quarter (twelve weeks), or a fee per credit hour, or a combination of charges where a period of time and a fixed charge per class is assessed. The least expensive are state and community-supported colleges. The most expensive are private schools. Typically, you may find that a twelve-week quarter of instruction will cost anywhere from a low of $75 at a state or community college to upwards of $1,000 at a private school. Additionally, you will be expected to pay for your books, for lab use, equipment, special clothes (if required), and for administrative costs such as health insurance as well as other activity charges. To these you will need to add costs for transportation, meals, and miscellaneous supplies.

Paying for Your Education

If you don't have unlimited funds, you will obviously need some assistance in paying for your education. There are many sources of financial assistance available. Which source you will be able to qualify for will depend on a number of factors. There are grants and loans based simply on your need: grants and loans based on your family's or your personal ability to pay; work-study programs that alternate employment within your chosen career field with classroom education; scholarships, grants, and awards for your academic accomplishments or potential; and local, state, federal, and private sources of financial aid.

The federal government has several financial aid packages:

1. Pell Grants. Established in 1980, these grants are based on your family's needs. The maximum amounts change each year.
2. Guaranteed Student Loans. This program supports or guarantees loans made to students by banks and savings and loan associations. The interest rate for these loans is quite reasonable and

repayment does not begin until after you have finished your education.

3. Supplemental Educational Opportunity Grants. This program awards grants, not loans, of up to $2,000 per year based on a student's financial need.

4. GI Bill. This educational training allowance is available to honorably discharged members of the U.S. Armed Forces and provides up to $28,000 for college-level training.

For students residing in states with lotteries, it's a good idea to check and see if there are any special programs for higher education financed in part by the proceeds. For example, a student residing in Georgia who maintained a B average in high school and whose parents earn less than $100,000 yearly qualifies for the HOPE scholarship program, which provides full tuition at any state university and up to $1,000 per year at a private school. This program may be available in some other form in other states, so it bears looking into.

There are numerous private, civic, and philanthropic sources of student aid. These books can be used to determine what is available in aid, the requirements, and how to apply:

Barron's Guide to Scholarships and Financial Aid (Woodbury, NY; Barron's Educational Series).

The College Money Handbook (Princeton, NJ; Peterson's Guides).

Dollars for Scholars Student Aid Catalogs (Princeton, NJ; Peterson's Guides). These are state-by-state guides to financial aid.

Financing College Education (New York; Harper Colophon Books).

Lovejoy's Guide to Scholarships and Grants (New York; Monarch Press).

A TYPICAL JUNIOR COLLEGE COURSE OUTLINE

No two colleges or vocational technical schools are the same. The course outline shown here is a rather typical outline for an eight-quarter, two-year program leading to an associate degree in electronics engineering technology that prepares the student for a career in computer maintenance. The differences between schools might involve elective courses such as English and the humanities. The eight-quarter course contains 152 units of instruction. We will look first at the program outline and then at the individual course descriptions. This course outline is courtesy of the Heald Institute of Technology, a private junior college located in San Jose, California.

ELECTRONIC ENGINEERING TECHNOLOGY
Course Outline

1st Quarter		Units
E110	Introduction to Electronics	10
E110L	Electronics Lab	2
M110	Algebra I	5
M110L	Mathematics Lab	2
		19

2nd Quarter		
E120	Circuit Analysis	10
E120L	Electronics Lab	4
M120	Algebra and Trigonometry	5
		19

3rd Quarter		
E130	Solid-State Circuits	15
E130L	Electronics Lab	4
		19

4th Quarter		
E240	Communications Circuits	10
E240L	Electronics Lab	4
D240	Programming I	5
		19

5th Quarter		
E250	Digital Circuits	10
E250L	Electronics Lab	4
D250	Programming II	5
		19

6th Quarter		
E260	Microprocessors	10
E260L	Electronics Lab	4
G260	Technical Communications	5
		19

7th Quarter		Units
E370	Microprocessor Systems	10
E370L	Electronics Lab	4
G370	Industrial Psychology	5
		19
8th Quarter		
E380	Communications Systems	8
E380L	Electronics Lab	4
E382	Electronic Systems	5
E384	Electronics Seminar	2
		19

Total: 8 Quarters, 152 Units, Associate of Science Degree

Course Descriptions

E110 *Introduction to Electronics.* Introduction to basic electrical concepts and principles of DC circuits including Ohm's law series circuits, parallel circuits, and series-parallel circuits.

E110L *Electronics Lab.* Taken with E110. Familiarization and use of tools, components, and instruments associated with direct current measurements. Introduction to circuit breadboarding and measurement techniques.

M110 *Algebra I.* Review of fundamentals of arithmetic and introduction to scientific notation and the basic concepts of algebra, including fundamental operations, linear equations in one variable, special products and factoring algebraic fractions, linear equations in two variables, and exponents and radicals.

M110L *Mathematics Lab.* Individualized problem-solving sessions in arithmetic and basic algebra.

E120L *Electronics Lab.* Operation and use of basic DC and AC measuring instruments are studied in detail. Laboratory exercises involve the design and construction of series-parallel circuits, loaded voltage dividers, and bridge circuits; verification of Kirchoff's laws; inductance and inductive reactance, capacitors and capacitive reactance, RC time constant, RL and RC circuits, series and parallel resonance and filters.

E120 *Circuit Analysis.* Review of basic principles of DC circuits and introduction to Kirchoff's laws and network theorems; magnetism; principles of alternating current circuits, including voltage, current inductance, capacitance, resonance, and transformers.

M120 *Algebra and Trigonometry.* Introduction to trigonometric functions, the solution of right angles, trigonometric identities, elementary plane vectors, phasor algebra, logarithms, quadradic equations, and the concepts of differential and integral calculus. Emphasis is on developing practical ability to solve electronic circuit problems.

E130 *Solid-State Circuits.* Review of network theorems and introduction to semiconductor theory, diodes and diode circuits, amplifiers, field effect transistors, and FET circuit analysis.

E130L *Electronics Lab.* Laboratory exercises with solid-state electronic devices and circuits including transistor characteristics, DC/AC equivalent circuits, and multistage amplifier design.

E240 *Communications Circuits.* Course is continuation of El30 and begins with oscillators, power supplies, and power amplifiers and leads to an introduction to the concepts of electronic systems. Emphasis is placed on the study of communications techniques and systems, including frequency response and the transfer characteristics of communications networks, signal and noise analysis, AM and FM, and pulse and pulse code modulation and applications.

E240L *Electronics Lab.* Supports the communications circuits course. Lab experiments provide practical experience in communications circuits and subsystems. Typical circuits are breadboarded, and performance measurements are made with a wide variety of instruments.

D240 *Programming I.* Introduction to high-level language programming. Students write, analyze, and execute programs to solve a variety of technically oriented problems.

E250 *Digital Circuits.* Introduction to digital circuits, including number systems, logic, Boolean Algebra, combination logic functions, binary arithmetic, multiplexers, flip-flops, counters, shift registers, tristate logic, memories and addressing, and data synchronization and interfacing.

E250L *Electronics Lab.* Experiments involve digital logic design, encoders and decoders, flip-flop counters, one-shots, memories, shift registers, and busing.

D250 *Programming II.* Course continues with emphasis given to technical applications of programming.

E260 *Microprocessors.* Introduction to microprocessor architecture, programming, and applications. Popular eight- and sixteen-bit microprocessors are studied in detail; developing technologies are discussed.

E260L *Electronics Lab.* Lab experiments include processing data inputs and outputs, processing and forming data arrays, designing and debugging assembly language programs, arithmetic, subroutines and stack usage, handshaking, interrupts, timing methods, serial input/output, peripheral interfacing, and examining processor signals.

G260 *Technical Communications.* Instruction and practice in the preparation of technically oriented reports and other kinds of writing based on the practical needs of technicians. Special attention is given to the problems of spelling, grammar, sentence structure, punctuation, and information organization and presentation.

E370 *Microprocessor Systems.* This course defines an operating system and its hardware and software requirements and shows how compatibility is achieved among its separate components. The functions of the interconnecting data, address, control, and status buses of a microcomputer are explained along with the necessary memory and I/O accessing techniques and devices.

E370L *Electronics Lab.* Lab exercises cover microprocessor interface circuits and system peripherals. Both hardware and software aspects are examined.

G370 *Industrial Psychology.* Introduction to the understanding of human behavior, especially as applied to situations characteristic of an industrial environment.

E380 *Communications Systems.* This sequence is devoted to communications systems including microwave, cellular radio and telephone

PBX, and packet-switching communications networks. Operation of, and testing procedures for, these systems are covered.

E380L *Electronics Lab.* Exercises at the system level for microwave, cellular radio, and telephone systems. Emphasis is on system operation and testing procedures.

E382 *Electronic Systems.* Investigates current applications of electronics for commercial and home systems including audiovisual systems, copier systems, and medical systems. Students study the mechanical as well as the electronic aspects of these systems.

E384 *Electronics Seminar.* Problem-solving seminar covering all aspects of electronics engineering technology; focuses on preparing the student for technical interviews and employment.

SUMMARY

If you were to refer back to the CBEMA guidelines earlier in this chapter, you could compare this typical course outline with the guidelines. Almost all of the requirements set forth by CBEMA are met in this eight-quarter course. The most obvious omission is the map reading, but it is a skill easily mastered. A course outline may vary from institution to institution, but the courses will remain the same. As a point of interest, at the time this book was being prepared, the tuition for this program, not counting books or lab fees, exceeded $12,500. It should be noted that the Heald Institute is a private, accredited, degree-granting institution. A similar program at a community or junior college might cost only about $5,000, or less, including books and lab fees. If money is of a concern, you should definitely check out the availability of local or state junior college programs where your tax dollars subsidize the cost of education.

FOR MORE INFORMATION

For more information about junior, community, or vocational technical schools in your area, you might want to consult your telephone directory under "schools" or ask your guidance counselor.

CHAPTER 4

MILITARY TRAINING

EARN WHILE YOU LEARN

For many years the U.S. Army, Air Force, Navy, Marines, and Coast Guard have provided a variety of training to people who elect to enlist in the service branch of their choice. During a tour of duty, which can be as short as two years or as long as six, enlistees are trained in a specialty and are paid while they learn. Additionally, unlike attending a junior college or vocational school, service-trained specialists receive experience on-the-job, actually performing the duties they have been trained for. You can either go to a college or vocational school and pay anywhere from $2,500 to $12,000 or more for your education, or you can invest two to six years of your time and receive training and experience and get paid at the same time. About 60 percent of all training in the modern military is other than in combat arms, thereby affording an enlistee the chance to learn skills and technology that can and do translate into a civilian occupational specialty.

Enlisting in the military isn't what your parents or relatives might lead you to believe. Compulsory military service, also known as the draft, no longer exists in the United States. All of the military services fill their requirements from the ranks of volunteers; because of this fact, as well as the excellent and upgraded salaries it offers, the military is somewhat "choosy." Minimum requirements for enlistment include a valid high school diploma, not a GED certificate. You must be either a U.S. citizen or be able to furnish proof that you are an alien who has been lawfully admitted to the United States for permanent residence.

You must also be not less than eighteen years of age at the time of your enlistment. If you are at least seventeen, a special form called DD 1966, Parental Consent, is required. In addition, your background is closely examined. If you have any criminal record, or more than a minor traffic infraction, you may not be able to enter the service of your choice, or for that matter, if you can enlist, your training options will be sorely limited. The military, like other federal employers, is an equal opportunity employer. With the exception of certain combat-related job fields, women can qualify for any of the hundreds of technical and vocational training programs without discrimination. In exchange for a commitment on your part to serve for anywhere from two to six years, the military will train you and provide you with housing, clothing, medical care, and the opportunity to work with some of the most sophisticated technology available. This is in addition to a salary that begins at more than $7,668 per year. The actual compensation value for the entry-level recruit, taking into account such allowances as those for dependents and housing, exceeds $12,000 per year.

ENTERING THE SERVICE OF YOUR CHOICE

You may have already been approached by representatives of the military about careers in their respective branches at high school job fairs or similar activities. Assuming that you are interested in a career in the military, your first stop will be at the local recruiter's office for that particular branch of the service. You can find these offices by looking in your phone book under the heading "U.S. Government." All of the services have essentially the same requirements. This section will examine the U.S. Army in depth, including some actual course outlines from various computer maintenance courses available to enlistees.

Once you have made an appointment with your local recruiter, you will be given a series of brochures explaining the various enlistment options and the available training, and you will be asked to take a test. This test, the AFQT (Armed Forces Qualification Test), determines where your skills, weaknesses, and strengths lie. It is an excellent method of determining in what fields the best chances of your success are located. The results of a sample pretest, given via interactive computer at a local army recruiter's office, appear on an upcoming page. This interesting quiz, called CAST (Computerized Adaptive Screening Test), enables the recruiter to quickly determine if you will be able to make the grade on the AFQT and ASVAB (Armed Services Vocational Aptitude Battery Test) before proceeding any further. The AFQT and ASVAB tests are the same regardless of the branch of service you choose.

Assuming you have, in the case of the army, successfully scored over fifty on this test, you will either take the AFQT and ASVAB tests at the recruiting center or be scheduled to take these tests along with a comprehensive medical exam at a special testing center. You will be furnished transportation, lodging, and meals if this testing center is not located in your hometown. You can take these tests and the medical exam and still have no obligation to enlist. These are merely screening tests to determine your suitability for military service. Many high school seniors take these tests prior to graduation as part of their overall career planning.

Once you have arrived at the testing center, you will take the AFQT and ASVAB tests. These tests measure your verbal and nonverbal skills, math abilities, and vocational interests. The tests require no preparation and serve as guides to where your career interests and abilities lie. Your medical examination follows these written tests. Trained medical personnel will evaluate you to ensure that you meet the minimum medical guidelines for military service. You will be tested for color blindness to ensure that you can distinguish different colors. If you fail this portion of the test, you will find that you will not be able to enter any of the high-technology training fields where you must be able to distinguish color-codes on components.

Assuming you pass the medical exam, your next stop will be with a career counselor who is specially trained to evaluate your test and medical scores and compare them with your career goals and military options. This counselor functions for the military in much the same manner as your high school career guidance counselor. The objective of the career counselor is to determine your aptitudes and help you channel your efforts toward meeting your career goals. In the case of the army, once you and your METS (military educational training specialist) representative have reviewed and evaluated your scores,

CONGRATULATIONS   87-08-26

You meet the preliminary aptitudinal requirements for enlistment in the U.S. Army.

The Computerized Adaptive Screening Test (CAST) predicts your probable Armed Forces Qualification Test (AFQT) score on the Armed Services Vocational Aptitude Battery Test (ASVAB). These computer test scores are no guarantee you will qualify on the actual ASVAB; however, based on an indepth study the CAST has a highly predictive AFQT accuracy. That is, there is a high probability that your ASVAB AFQT will be the same as your CAST AFQT.

Your Computerized Adaptive Screening Test results are as follows:

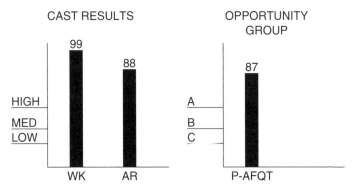

A printout of this information is provided to you. This information is electronically stored on a microcomputer diskette, where it can be retrieved and transcribed onto recruiting and enlistment forms as applicable.

This printout is not a contract and in no way obligates you or the Army.

THIS IS NOT A CONTRACT

you will be presented with a list of army career fields that your interests and the results of your tests show you are best qualified to pursue. Each of these fields will have corresponding educational and training schedules, and you will be able to view video presentations of actual classroom and on-the-job activities. In fact, prior to making any commitment to the military, you will be asked to sign a paper stating that you have viewed this material so that there will be no chance of any misunderstanding. The army and, to a great extent, the other branches of the military enter into a legal binding contract with an enlistee specifying what training and assignments this person has specifically enlisted for. If either party fails in their obligations, the contract can be terminated.

Having satisfied the educational and medical requirements, you are ready to enlist. You must, however, meet the requirements for the specific field you elect and contract to train in. You must meet the age requirement and successfully complete the background investigation, at which time you will be issued a legal and binding contract spelling out the commitment on the part of the army and the commitment on your own part. The agreement will spell out where and when your training will take place and for how long. Additionally, you might even be able to negotiate a duty assignment location. Again, until you take the oath, you have no obligation for military service. Assuming that you have completed high school and are ready, you will report to a processing center, take the oath, and begin your military career.

BASIC TRAINING

Before you can become a technical specialist, the military requires that you learn to be a soldier. You will be sent to a basic training center and for the next two months learn what the military is all about. You will learn discipline and how to march, and you will receive training in small arms, tactics, physical fitness, and other military-related subjects. You must remember that despite your career goals, you are a member of the military and must be trained accordingly. During basic training, you will also receive your uniforms and perhaps for the first time in your life know exactly what you will be wearing each and every day, and for that matter, what everyone around you will be wearing—basic army green! You will be receiving your first army pay, and before you know it graduation day will arrive as will your assignment to your technical training.

TECHNICAL TRAINING

The military uses vast amounts of high-technology equipment in offices—and in battlefields. Some of the computer-related systems ride aboard battle tanks, others fly faster than the speed of sound, and still others are submerged below the ocean's surface on submarines. Regardless of the location of this complex array of equipment, someone must be available and trained to provide technical service to it. Training on this equipment lasts for at least fifteen weeks and, more likely than not, can extend to the better part of a year, especially if you can qualify for advanced training. Let's look at some of the typical training available in the army's computer maintenance field. All of these courses are taught at Fort Gordon, Georgia.

TACTICAL COMPUTER SYSTEMS REPAIRER

The objective of this twenty-week course is to train enlisted personnel in the fundamentals of automatic data processing equipment and the skills required to troubleshoot, repair, and maintain a tactical computer system. Its scope covers maintenance, troubleshooting, and repair of tactical computer systems, including processors, console panels, memory units, power supplies, magnetic tape units, keyboards, disk memory units, printers, and modems. Class size is limited to twelve, and 720 academic hours of training are provided.

OCCUPATIONAL SPECIALTY CODE 39T10
Course Summary

Course Title	Hours
Basic Electronic Fundamentals	64
Solid-State Power Supplies	61

Course Title	Hours
Practical, Perform Executive Commands and Utilities on Tactical Computer	70
Practical, Perform System Diagnostics	49
Practical, Troubleshoot Tactical Computer Data Communications	87
Practical, Troubleshoot Peripherals of the Tactical Computer System	56
Practical, Perform Cabling, System Initialization, and Data Communications Using the Tactical Computer Terminal	36
Practical, Troubleshoot and Repair Peripherals of the Tactical Computer Terminal	154
Practical, Troubleshoot and Repair the Tactical Logistic Applications of Automated Marking and Reading Symbols	36
Practical, Troubleshoot and Repair the Unit Level Computer	36
Common Precision Soldering Course	42
End of Course Comprehensive Exam	18
Mandatory Training Annex	11

INTERMEDIATE-LEVEL MAINTENANCE AUTOMATIC TEST SYSTEM

The objective of this eighteen-week course is to provide enlisted personnel who have already qualified in occupational specialty code 39B with skills and knowledge necessary to perform intermediate-level maintenance on the automatic test system AN/MSM-105 (V) 1. The course's scope covers troubleshooting the test facility using manual fault isolation procedures when the internal self-diagnostic program fails. It also covers repairs to automatic test equipment by removing and replacing major assemblies, subassemblies, printed circuit boards, wiring harnesses, and cables. Training includes inspecting and checking maintenance performed for quality and suitability. This automated test system is used to diagnose and repair the computer-controlled systems used on modern military helicopters. The maximum class size is limited to twelve, with 686 hours of academic training.

INTERMEDIATE LEVEL MAINTENANCE
Course Summary

Course Title	Hours
DC Fundamentals	81
Basic Logic Circuits	64
Combined Logic Functions	94
Practical, Troubleshooting the Digital Card Tester	66
Practical, Troubleshooting the Computer Control Group	46
Practical, Troubleshooting the Stimulus Subsystems	99
Practical, Troubleshooting the System Interface Units	47
Practical, Troubleshooting the Measurement Subsystems	79
Practical, Troubleshooting the RF/Microwave Subsystems	74
AN/MSM-105 (V) 1 System Repair and End-of-Course Comprehensive Test	33
Mandatory Training Including Academic Physical Fitness	3

DAS3 COMPUTER SYSTEMS REPAIRER

This twenty-seven-week course's objective is to train enlisted personnel in the fundamentals of automatic data processing equipment and the skills and knowledge necessary to troubleshoot, repair, and maintain the decentralized automated service support systems computer systems. Its scope includes maintenance, troubleshooting, and repairs to console panels, processors, memory units, power supplies, card reader/punch and controller, magnetic tape units, disk memory units, keyboards, printers, and modems. Class size is limited to a maximum of fourteen, with a total of 1,025 academic hours.

OCCUPATIONAL SPECIALTY CODE 39D
Course Summary

Course Title	Hours
Basic Electronic Fundamentals	64
Solid-State Power Supplies	62
Computer Fundamentals	90

Course Title	Hours
Practical, Test/Troubleshoot Video Display Terminal	30
Practical, Test/Troubleshoot Console Printers	42
Practical, Test/Troubleshoot Line Printer RP-273	28
Practical, Test/Troubleshoot Line Printer RP-309	30
Practical, Test/Troubleshoot Card Punch Reader Interpreters	122
Practical, Test/Troubleshoot Magnetic Tape Unit	30
Practical, Test/Troubleshoot Disk Memory Unit	46
Practical, Test/Troubleshoot Data Processing Unit	76
Practical, Van Maintenance	136
Practical, Test/Operate/Troubleshoot CP-1435A/MYQ-4 and Remote Subsystems OL-341/MYQ4A and OA-9192/MYQ-4a	106
Practical, Test/Operate/Troubleshoot Link Communications System	100
Practical, Troubleshoot AN/MYQ-4A System	59
Practical, Physical Fitness Training, Equal Opportunity, and Prevention of Sexual Harassment	4

SUMMARY

Although only representative outlines of three army courses have been presented, there are many opportunities in the high-technology computer-related maintenance field in all of the armed forces. The military offers you the unique opportunity to learn your skill, to be paid while you learn, and to gain the valuable experience that employers are looking for. In addition, as a member of the military, you will be eligible for advanced educational opportunities while in service at local or on-base educational centers, and you will be able to participate in the new GI Bill, which could, with your contribution of $1,200, entitle you to up to $25,200 in allowances for use in furthering your education. The military is both a source of training and a career employer. As a member of the military, you receive an excellent salary, benefits comparable to private industry, and the opportunity for retirement at the end of only twenty years of service. On the other hand, the rigorous discipline and frequent moves associated with military life may not be your life's goal. But the military does provide a viable opportunity for you to learn your chosen career, gain invaluable work experience, and amass savings toward furthering your education. It merits your consideration. If college or the military isn't in your immediate future, home or correspondence study or self-directed study may meet your requirements. These options will be explored in the next chapter.

FOR MORE INFORMATION

You can obtain more information from your local military recruiter, whose address and telephone number can be found in your local telephone directory under the heading "U.S. Government."

CHAPTER 5

CORRESPONDENCE COURSES

Simply defined, home or correspondence study is enrollment with an educational institution that provides lesson materials prepared in a sequential and logical order for study by students on their own. When each lesson is completed, the student mails the assigned work to the school for correction, grading, comment, and subject-matter guidance by qualified instructors. There may also be combination courses that provide some training in-residence for students who complete their home study lessons. Some institutions offer diploma courses, and others have been authorized and approved to award associate degrees in applied science and electronics technology to successful graduates. More frequently than not, specialized experiments, kits, and supplies supplement the course material, enabling a student to obtain practical hands-on experience.

Home study and self-study are different. Self-study, or self-directed education, relies on only the student and self-study materials. There is no feedback from an instructor, affiliation with a school, or special help if and when you need it. However, for the motivated person, much can be gained from self-directed study.

In the high-technology field, home or correspondence study has been around since the birth of radio. Initially, correspondence training was the only method of educating electronics pioneers in great numbers. It originally consisted of lessons, tests, and experiments centered around technology as it existed in 1916. Like the technology, it has grown, incorporating the latest advances and adding courses that are up-to-date and directly related to occupational requirements. The government—or more specifically, the military—both uses and produces correspondence courses for service personnel throughout the world.

According to information furnished by the National Home Study Council, more than fifty million Americans have taken advantage of home study or correspondence courses since 1890. These courses have covered the entire educational spectrum from horseshoeing through the very latest in high technology. Each year an estimated three million Americans study something via correspondence. These people from all walks of life study to improve themselves and to get ahead. Home or correspondence study is selected because it has been found to be a practical, convenient, and economical way to get training and education. Home or correspondence study institutions also can provide a second opportunity for those whose educations were interrupted for one reason or another.

For some people, college or available military training is out of the question. Perhaps you live too far from a school or don't have the time to attend classes or maybe you have a physical handicap that restricts your mobility. In such cases, home or correspondence study may be your key to obtaining the training to qualify for a career in computer maintenance. As a student you will be in a class by yourself. You will progress at your own pace without being forced to hurry through material or wait until slower students catch up. You can study at a schedule convenient to you, with a quiet area in your home as your classroom. School can begin when you have returned from a job, before you go to work, or on weekends. Additionally, all of the schools listed at the end of this chapter have some form of time payment plan to finance your education over a period of years, either in monthly or quarterly payments.

A TYPICAL STUDENT PROFILE

According to the staff of the National Radio Institute, one of the oldest correspondence schools in the United States, 60 percent of all students enrolled in microcomputer and microprocessor technology courses are between the ages of 18 and 35, with a reported 20.5 percent of these same students being between the ages of 18 and 25. Educationally, 37 percent have at least a high school diploma, 36 percent have between one to three years of college, and 20 percent are college graduates. Nearly one-fourth of the students surveyed are currently working in electronics or computer-related fields. When asked for their reasons for enrolling in the course, 97 percent responded that they enrolled for career growth. More than one-half of all students were reported to be married, and approximately 6 percent of the student body were identified as female.

COURSE AND PROGRAM CONTENT

This chapter will examine the available courses and their contents and will conclude with a profile of a graduate of one of these courses. For the purpose of our examination, we will look at a diploma course and also at a course that leads to an associate degree. Regardless of the degree or diploma course, you will find that all of these programs consist of well-written text materials requiring a maximum of interaction on your part, specific experiments and kits to reinforce the subject matter, and frequent examinations to validate the learning process. As compared to resident-school training, which could run upwards of $10,000, home or correspondence study programs range from about $900 to $6,000, depending on the scope and amount of equipment, kits, and materials furnished. However, it's important to keep in mind that these tuition rates are all inclusive; there are no other fees, no textbook or lab charges.

NONDEGREE PROGRAM MICROCOMPUTERS AND MICROPROCESSOR TECHNOLOGY INCLUDING IBM-COMPATIBLE COMPUTER

This course consists of forty-nine lessons, with a total of nine action learning kits including an IBM-compatible personal computer and hardware. The course is designed to prepare the student for a career as a bench or field computer maintenance specialist. It is estimated that the average student will complete this course in eighteen to twenty-four months.

Course Outline

Lesson	Title
1	Introduction to Computer Electronics
2	How Electricity Is Produced for Electronics
3	Current, Voltage, and Resistance
4	Series Circuits
5	Parallel Circuits
6	How Resistors Are Used
7	How Coils Are Used
8	How Capacitors Are Used
9	How Coils and Capacitors Are Used Together
10	How Diodes Work
11	How Transistors Work
12	How Transistors Are Used
13	Integrated Circuits
14	Power Supplies for Electronic Equipment
15	How Amplifiers Work
16	How Oscillators Work
17	Periodic Waves and Time Constants
18	Relays and Relay Circuits
19	Introduction to Computers
20	How Computers Are Used
21	Basic Computer Arithmetic
22	Digital Codes and Computer Arithmetic
23	Digital Logic Circuits
24	Boolean Algebra and Digital Logic
25	Flip-flops, Registers, and Counters
26	How Digital Logic Is Used
27	Computer Arithmetic Operations
28	How Digital Computers Operate
29	Register Transfers and Addressing
30	Computer Memories
31	Computer Input/Output
32	Computer Peripheral Equipment
33	Data Conversion Systems
34	Data Communications and Peripherals
35	Microprocessors and Microcomputers
36	Microcomputer Applications

Lesson   Title

In addition to the forty-nine lessons, a total of nine kits are furnished to reinforce materials learned from the text. These kits consist of the following:

1. Transistors, resistors, and LED to enable the student to build actual circuits, observe the effects of changing resistance or voltage, and better understand series and parallel circuits.

2. A handheld, 3 1/2-digit, digital voltmeter to be used in experiments to perform a variety of measurements.

3. Hardware kit to supplement the study of AC circuits and enable the student to build a power supply and examine the effects of inductance and resonance.

4. A specially designed power supply and the first phase of a Discovery Lab that the student builds and uses to examine the operation of power supplies, rectifiers, and filtering circuits.

5. The final and major assembly phase of the Discovery Lab, which will be used for a series of experiments and observations to reinforce the study of solid-state electronics.

6. An introduction to, and the use of, integrated circuits as well as transistors to illustrate analog and digital logic circuits in conjunction with the text and the Discovery Lab.

7. A hardware kit consisting of the power supply and the intelligent keyboard for the microcomputer furnished with the course. Experiments guide the student through the techniques of measurement as well as building a digital logic probe from supplied parts.

An 8-LED test fixture is built to enable testing of the computer's intelligent keyboard. Parts are used to construct a serial data receiver circuit to view the signals and data generated by the keyboard.

8. A kit containing the computer cabinet, cooling fan, main logic board, disk drive, twelve-inch monochrome video display, interconnecting cables, and MS-DOS operating system diskette. Experiments include examination of circuitry on main logic board, assembly of the computer, and testing procedures.

9. Special exercises in programming using MS-DOS and assembly language designed to reinforce text materials as well as gain an understanding as to how the computer processes information.

ASSOCIATE DEGREE PROGRAM
INCLUDING TRAINING AND TEST EQUIPMENT

This comprehensive, 246-lesson course carries 106 credit hours. It features 397 experiments using a microprocessor training laboratory, a personal training laboratory, multimeter, digital security control device, and oscilloscope. The course has three supervised examinations and requires the student to prepare and submit five technical papers. The maximum time allowed to complete this course is forty-eight months. The structure of the course is identical to those courses leading to associate degrees found in community or private junior colleges. The only major difference is the lack of a requirement for residency.

A full complement of mathematics courses are included as are introductory courses in physics. The course structure has been designed to meet or exceed the guidelines set forth by CBEMA. Detailed course outlines as well as information on enrollment can be obtained by writing directly to the Cleveland Institute of Electronics. The address is found at the end of this chapter. The course tuition, including all texts and training materials is $6,000, payable in full or in eight installments of $750 each.

A.A.S. CORRESPONDENCE SCHOOL COURSE LIST

The following list of the courses in a degree-level program of instruction in electronics engineering technology is reprinted courtesy of the Cleveland Institute of Electronics.

- Current and Voltage
- Controlling Current and Voltage
- Power Distribution
- Portable Extension Cords
- Static Electricity
- Electric Currents and Semiconductor Devices
- Fractions and Decimal Numbers
- Reciprocals, Percentage, and Powers of Numbers
- The Three Basics of Electric Circuits: Voltage, Current, and Resistance
- Ohm's Law, Conductors, and Insulators
- Connecting and Tracing Battery Circuits
- Identifying Components
- Tracing Wiring on Printed Circuit Boards
- Roots of Numbers, Ratio, and Proportion
- Inverse Proportion and Negative Numbers
- Parallel Circuits
- Equivalent Circuits
- Applications of Kirchhoff's Laws
- Series-Parallel Circuits
- Voltage and Power
- Vital Statistics of AC Circuits
- Magnetism and Magnetic Circuits
- Induced Voltage and Current
- Elements of Logic
- Logic Circuits
- Scientific Notation
- Units of Measure
- Inductance
- Mutual Inductance and Magnetic Coupling
- Transformers
- Reliable Soldering Techniques
- Working with Printed Circuit Boards
- Building a Siren with Flashing Light
- Electrical Charges and Capacitance
- Capacitors in Action
- Rectifiers and Amplifiers

- Transistor and FET Amplifiers
- Reading and Using Graphs
- Phasors and Formulas
- Using Your Multimeter to Measure Resistance
- Your Personal Training Laboratory
- Series and Parallel Resistor Circuits
- Power and DC Circuits
- Simplifying Circuit Analysis by Using Kirchhoff's Laws
- Practical Applications of Kirchhoff's Laws
- Currents and Voltages in AC Circuits
- Capacitors and Capacitive Circuits
- Resonant Circuits
- Inductors and Inductive Circuits
- Resonance and Filters
- Using Semiconductor Diodes
- Operation of Semiconductor Devices
- Working with Semiconductor Diodes
- Unregulated Power Supplies
- Operation of Tubes and Transistors
- Amplifier Circuitry
- Fundamentals of Transformers
- Unregulated Power Supply Characteristics
- How to Work with Transistors
- Transistors Part I
- Common-Emitter Amplifier Characteristics
- Transistors Part II
- Audio Amplifiers and Equipment
- Operational Amplifiers
- Operational Amplifier Characteristics
- Silicon-Controlled Rectifiers and Unijunction Transistors: Theory and Applications
- Regulated Power Supplies
- Regulated Power Supply Characteristics
- Working with FETs
- Radio-Frequency Amplifiers
- Oscillators
- Sinusoidal Oscillators

- Measuring and Measuring Instruments
- Measurement Techniques Laboratory
- Circuit Response to Non-Sinusoidal Waveforms
- Time Constants
- RC Filter Circuits
- Understanding and Using the Oscilloscope
- Optoelectronics
- Digital Switching Units
- Binary Coding and Computer Arithmetic
- Logic Circuit Tracing by Using Boolean Algebra
- Digital IC Families with Practical Operating Requirements
- Clippers, Clampers, and Binaries
- Pulse Processing Circuits
- Multivibrators
- Important Digital Integrated Circuits
- 555 Timing Circuits
- Digital Systems and How to Troubleshoot Them
- Electromagnetism and Relays
- Systematic Troubleshooting
- Basic Gates
- Practical Digital Circuits
- Sequential Logic Circuits
- Safety
- Introduction to Television
- The Television System-Functional Block Diagram
- Television Troubleshooting Techniques
- Power Supplies
- Horizontal Circuits
- High-Voltage Circuits
- Vertical Circuits
- Tuners
- Intermediate-Frequency Amplifiers
- Video Circuits and the CRT
- AGC Circuits
- Synchronization Circuits
- Introduction to Color Television
- Color Circuits

- Color Symptom Troubleshooting
- Color TV Setup
- Sound Circuits
- Advanced Troubleshooting Techniques
- Introduction to Digital Electronics
- Number Systems
- Fundamentals of Boolean Algebra
- Karnaugh Maps
- NOR and NAND Gate Circuits
- Discrete Logic Gates
- Digital Integrated Circuits
- Digital Flip-Flops
- One-Shots, Astables, and Schmitt Triggers
- Counter Design
- Modulus Counters
- Shift Registers and Counters
- Binary Codes and Converters
- Multiplexers-Demultiplexers
- CMOS Digital Logic
- Digital Interfacing Circuits
- ROMS, PROMS, and PLAs
- Introduction to Computers and Microprocessors
- Oscilloscope Measurements
- Oscilloscope Triggering
- Oscilloscope Analysis of Analog and Digital Circuits
- Supervised Examination
- Solving Linear Equations
- Algebraic Signs and Exponents
- Kirchhoff's Laws
- Kirchhoff's Laws Laboratory
- Increasing Your Understanding of Kirchhoff's Laws
- Algebraic Fractions
- Applied Fractional Equations
- Basic Circuit Principles Applied to Practical Design
- Basic Design Laboratory
- Network Theorems
- Dual Circuits Laboratory

- Superposition
- Coordinates and Angle Functions
- Applications of Trigonometric Functions
- Exponents, Radicals, and Complex Numbers
- Phasor Representation of Steady-State Circuits
- Analytic Geometry: First Degree Equations
- Some Basic Concepts of Calculus
- Signal Waveforms and Their Amplification
- Introduction to Solid-State Design Part I
- Advanced Network Theorems
- Advanced Network Theorems Laboratory Part I
- Advanced Network Theorems Laboratory Part II
- Diode Networks
- Introduction to Solid-State Design Part II
- Introduction to Solid-State Design Part III
- Ohm's and Kirchhoff's Laws Applied to AC Circuits
- AC Circuit Analysis
- AC Power and Solving Stage Coupling Problems
- AC Networks Laboratory
- Resonant Circuits
- Systems of Linear Equations
- Linear Network Analysis
- Simplifying Network Analysis by Using Determinants
- Practical Matrix Theory for Engineers
- Two-Port Linear Networks
- Quadratic Equations and Systems
- Higher Order Equations
- Trigonometric Equations and Identities
- Theory of Logarithms and Series
- Natural Logarithms
- PC Board Layout
- Calculus
  Part I—Analytic Geometry—Second Degree Equations
  Part II—Basic Concepts in Differential Calculus
  Part III—Further Differential Techniques and Applications of
     the Derivative
  Part IV—Fundamentals of Integration

Part V—Applying Integral Calculus
Part VI—Derivatives of Transcendental Functions
Part VII—Integrating Transcendental Functions
Part VIII—Series Representations and Indeterminate Forms
Part IX—Fourier Series and Differential Equations

- Transient Analysis Part I
- Transient Analysis Part II
- Transient Analysis Part III
- Transient Analysis Part IV
- Transient Analysis Part V
- Transient Analysis Part VI
- Diode Networks Laboratories
- Semiconductor Power Switching & Control Devices
- Bipolar Transistor Design Laboratory Part I
- Bipolar Transistor Design Laboratory Part II
- Field-Effect Transistors
- FET Design Laboratory
- Linear Integrated Circuits
- Operational Amplifier Laboratory
- Phase Locked Loops
- Active Filters
- Transducers
- Signal Flow Analysis
- General Feedback Principles
- Control Systems
- Data Transmission
- Basic Physics
- Physics of Mechanics
- Static Magnetic Field Theory
- Electric Field Physics
- Magnetic Circuits
- Optics and Heat
- Registers
- Arithmetic Logic Units
- Timing and Control
- Memory Units
- Supervised Examination

- Using the CIE 6809 Micro Trainer
- Number Systems and Data Codes
- Digital Arithmetic and Logic Operations
- The 6809 Architecture and Operation
- Programming I—Straight Line
- Programming H—Branches and Jumps
- Programming III—Stacks and Subroutines
- Programming IV—I/O and Interrupts
- Program Design and Testing
- Semiconductor Memory Interfacing
- The PIA and I/O
- Output: Displays and Sound
- Input: Switches/Keyboards
- Interrupt Systems
- Serial I/O: ACIA/UARTs
- Analog I/O: D/A and A/D Conversion
- Higher-Level Language: FORTRAN
- Overview of Reports: Your Options
- The Memorandum: Handling Frequent Writing Tasks
- Outlining the Short Report: A Planning Formula
- Audience Analysis: Remembering the Reader
- The Discussion: Report Designs that Succeed
- Graphics: Adding Information and Interest Visually
- Research and Resources: Gathering and Using Information
- Putting It All Together: A Short Report
- Design Standards for Writing: Grammar That Works
- Debugging the Report: Editing Business Letters
- Business Letters
- The Formal Report
- Investigation Reports
- Project and Progress Reports
- Proposals: Presenting the Evidence
- Written and Oral Presentations: Selling Yourself, Your Service,
  Your Product
- Papers:
  A Short Report
  A Business Letter

An Investigation Report
Project and Progress Report
Final Paper
- Supervised Examination
- Associate-Level CET Study Guide (Optional lessons at no
    extra charge)

SOMETHING TO THINK ABOUT

Although both of the programs we have examined will prepare you
for a career in computer maintenance, you will need both motivation
and a strong sense of self-discipline in order to succeed in either of
these two correspondence courses. There will be no teacher prodding
you to study. You will be on your own, alone in your "class of one."
You will have the advantage of being able to study when it's convenient
to your personal schedule, but you will have to make a schedule that
includes your studies. Additionally, if you elect to finance the cost of
your education, you will be entering into a legal and binding agreement
that will require you to make payments on a regular schedule. There
are obviously some distinct advantages, and likewise some shortcom-
ings. If you can discipline yourself into allocating a fixed time each
day and apply yourself to your studies, then your chances of success
are as good, if not better, than someone who attends a resident educational institution. However, if you become lax and let your studies slip,
you will have no one but yourself to blame.

Bob's Profile

Bob was scheduled to retire from the U.S. Marines after a career of
twenty-two years. During his military service, Bob was trained in the
combat arms, a field with little or no immediate use once his retirement
from the corps took place. About a year before his scheduled retirement, Bob used his GI Bill to enroll in a correspondence course in
microprocessor and computer technology. He'd learned as a forward
observer that computers and computer technology would obviously be
the way to go as far as a civilian career was concerned.

Bob's course gave him both theory and practical hands-on experience. He didn't have any trouble scheduling his studies around his normal schedule. Years in the military had instilled a sense of self-discipline in him and he found himself completing the course ahead of schedule. The computer furnished with the course gave him the opportunity to put many of the things he'd learned to good use. The result was an interview and job offer from a microcomputer manufacturer.

In fact this offer came from the company that contracted to supply the training microcomputer Bob had built as part of his training. His correspondence school training, combined with his military experience as a leader, earned Bob a position as a production line test supervisor on the same product line he'd studied in his course. Bob was responsible for a production line of twenty employees and served as the senior technical specialist for all quality control and quality assurance for that product. As a production line test supervisor, Bob's starting salary was in excess of $25,000 a year. Bob wouldn't recommend home study to just anyone. According to him, if you have the ability to set aside a fixed number of hours each day, go for it; if you have any doubts in your own self-discipline, try a resident program.

FOR MORE INFORMATION

You may wish to write to the schools listed below for more information about correspondence or home-study courses:

National Radio Institute
   3939 Wisconsin Avenue
   Washington, DC 20016

Cleveland Institute of Electronics
   1776 East Seventeenth Street
   Cleveland, OH 44114

National Technical Schools
   456 West Martin Luther King Jr. Boulevard
   Los Angeles, CA 90037-9988

CHAPTER 6

SELF-DIRECTED STUDY

DESIGNING YOUR OWN COURSE OF STUDY

There's quite a bit in common between correspondence training and self-directed study. In both cases you are alone in a class made up of only you, and it's up to you to decide that school will start at a fixed time each and every day. In the case made by the Home Study Council, the correspondence or home study course does offer an affiliation with an institution, feedback, and counsel. But self-directed study can provide a good practical and theoretical education that could prepare you for a career in computer maintenance. That doesn't mean that you can get a batch of books from the library, read them, and apply for a job. It means that you can structure an individual course of instruction using existing materials and supplemental experiments available from such companies as the Heath Company of Benton Harbor, Michigan.

Heath has an Educational Development Group that produces quality, self-paced instructional materials in many of the high-technology fields. In fact, this same group designed the courses used by many of the correspondence schools for training personnel on microcomputers and robotics. Obviously, you can't go wrong with the same educational materials some of the correspondence schools use. In addition, you can receive CEUs (continuing education units), a numerical value assigned to a specific educational course, which can be translated into college level credits at many community and junior colleges.

By designing your own course of instruction, you can cover those areas you do not know or are already proficient in, and you can concentrate on those areas that you need in order to satisfy the CBEMA guidelines. Eliminating the overhead present at the home study or correspondence school level can also amount to some substantial dollar savings for you. This can be important, especially if you are personally responsible for each and every educational dollar you spend. Each of the courses has a test that you can mail to Heath to be graded. A satisfactory grade earns you a certificate and a fixed number of CEUs.

You might wonder how you'd go about structuring your own study program. The work has already been done for you because many of the community and junior colleges use the very same materials and training experiments for their own programs. It's merely an exercise in picking those courses you require, sending in an order, waiting for delivery, and beginning your education. Let's examine some of the courses specifically designed to meet your career goals. At the end of the course description, we will total up the current costs of these programs and their accompanying experiments, labs, and accessories. Almost all of these courses are geared to experimenter's labs and may require you to purchase test equipment, hand tools, and other accessories. These requirements will be noted at the end of each course description. If money is tight or you only need certain courses, then self-directed study might just be for you.

DESCRIPTION OF COURSES

Typical Course Outline for Self-Directed Study
Computer Servicing & Advanced Microprocessing
Per CBEMA Educational Guidelines

(Course outlines and information courtesy of Heath Company, Benton Harbor, Michigan.)

THE FUNDAMENTALS

(Course Number, Title, and Description)

EI-3133 *Soldering.* A self-paced training course that will teach you professional soldering techniques utilizing a combination of text material and practical experiments. Requires a soldering iron and hand tools.

EE-3101-B *DC Electronics*. A self-paced course designed to acquaint you with basic principles of direct current electricity. Course material includes sections on current, voltage, resistance, Ohm's law, magnetism, electrical measurement techniques, DC circuits, inductance, and capacitance. You will use furnished parts to experiment with and build DC circuits and learn to draw schematics from a wiring diagram. Successful completion earns 2.0 CEUs. Requires the use of a multimeter, and ET-3600 Analog Trainer is highly recommended (trainer will be used for other courses as well).

EE-3102-B *AC Electronics*. A self-paced course complete with experiments to enable you to understand the principles of alternating current and its special applications in electronic circuits. Through experiments you will learn how various components react in AC circuits and see the application and use of AC components. Experiments include RC circuits, RL circuits, transformer characteristics, LC filters, and other associated projects. Successful completion of this course earns 1.5 CEUs. Requires the use of a multimeter and oscilloscope. ET-3600 Analog Trainer highly recommended.

EE-3103-B *Semiconductor Devices*. Self-paced course with experiments designed to expand on basic knowledge with an in-depth study of semiconductors, their properties, and use. Learning in a step-by-step manner, you will explore solid-state devices such as diodes, transistors, FETs, thyristors, and integrated circuits. The text and experiments allow you to learn the proper use and application of solid-state devices including precautions when handling. Course materials also cover the electrical characteristics of these components, how they are made, and how they operate in the microsized world of solid-state high technology. Successful completion of this course earns 3.0 CEUs. Requires the use of a multimeter and the ET-3600 Trainer.

EE-3104-B *Electronic Circuits*. Self-paced training program consisting of seven carefully designed educational units to lead the student from basic circuit concepts to fully designed circuitry found in everyday electronic products. Information enabling you to identify and understand power supply components, radio circuitry, regulatory circuits, amplifiers, and oscillators are among the course's contents. Over one hundred electronic components are included for use in fourteen experiments to reinforce and illustrate electronic circuit principles. Successful completion of this course earns 4.0 CEUs. Requires a multimeter, oscilloscope, and ET-3600 Trainer.

EE-3201-A *Digital Techniques.* This two-volume, self-paced training program starts off with the fundamentals and theory of digital logic, including number systems. Lesson materials aid the student in the design and application of modern digital circuitry. Students will become familiar with Boolean Algebra, flip-flops, registers, sequential logic circuits, combination logic circuits, and digital design. Course comes complete with all components necessary to perform twenty-four experiments reinforcing text materials and fundamentals. Successful completion of the course earns 4.0 CEUs. Requires a multimeter, oscilloscope, and the ET-3700 Digital Trainer.

ADVANCED TRAINING

Once you have mastered the basics, it's time to proceed to the subject of computer servicing and advanced microprocessing. A total of four educational programs cover this field. We will present the course titles, a brief description, and the course outlines for the three courses relating directly to computer servicing. The remaining course, titled Advanced Microprocessors, would be optional and could be taken after you have entered the field. Any required test equipment or trainers not already listed previously will follow the applicable course.

EC-2001 *Computer Servicing Fundamentals.* An eight-unit self-paced training course on the fundamentals of computers with an emphasis on microcomputers. Introductory material includes both eight- and sixteen-bit microprocessors, busing and interfacing CPUs, semiconductor memories, and an introduction to programming.

Course Outline

Unit 1. Computer Systems

Unit Introduction
Unit Objectives

Computer Basics
  Computer Operation
  Hardware—Keyboards and Displays
  The Stored Program Concept
  CPU Word Size
  Computer Architecture
  Bus Designs
Computer Applications
  Word Processing
  Data Processing
  Networks
  Scientific and Engineering Applications
  Education and Training
  Point of Sales Systems
  Entertainment and Home Use
Computer Systems
  Typical Hardware
  Input Devices
  Output Devices
  I/O Devices
  Mass Storage Devices
  Random Access Storage Devices
  Power Supplies
  ET-100 Hardware
  Typical Software
  ET-100 Software

Unit 2. Power Supplies

Unit Introduction
Unit Objectives
Computer Power Supplies
  LC Power Supplies
  Switching Power Supplies
  High Voltage Power Supplies
Power Conditioning and Filtering
  What is EMI?
  Power Line Conditioning

Power Supplies
  The Switching Power Supply
  ET-100 Power Supply

Unit 3. The Central Processing Unit

Unit Introduction
Unit Objectives
CPU Architecture
  What is a CPU?
  CPU Busing
  Buffers and Buffering
  CPU Interfacing
  CPU Operation
CPU Hardware
  8-bit Microprocessors
  8/16-bit CPUs
  16-bit Microprocessors
  Multiple chip CPUs

Unit 4. Support Circuitry

Unit Introduction
Unit Objectives
Reset Circuits
  Power-Up and Operator Resets
Timing Circuits
  Clocks
  Counters
  Delay Devices
Other Support Circuits
  Encoders
  Decoders
  Multiplexers
  Latches
  Specialized Circuits

Unit 5. Memory

Unit Introduction
Unit Objectives

Handling I/O
  Memory Mapped I/O
  Port-Addressed I/O
Data Communication
  Parallel I/O
  Serial I/O
  I/O Standards
Interface Circuits
  Peripheral Interface Adapters
  Universal Asynchronous Receivers/Transmitters
  Universal Synchronous/Asynchronous Receiver/Transmitters
ET-100 I/O
  Programmable Peripheral Interfaces
  ET-100 Ports

Unit 7. The Software Interface—1

Unit Introduction
Unit Objectives
Program Design
  Programming Objectives
  Flowcharts
Programming Languages
  Machine Language
  Assembly Language
Assemblers and Editors
  Assemblers
  Editors
  Editor/Assemblers
Debugging
  Error Types
  Error Detection and Correction
  Debuggers
  Debug Commands

Unit 8. The Software Interface—2

Unit Introduction
Unit Objectives

Hih-Level Languages
  Compilers
  Interpreters
Using Compilers
  Introduction to FORTRAN, COBOL, and PASCAL
Programming with Compilers
Using Interpreters
  Introduction to BASIC
Requires an ET-100 Microcomputer Trainer, cassette tape recorder, video monitor or television receiver with RF modulator. A dot-matrix printer, Epson MX-80 or equal, is helpful but not required.

EC-2002 *Computer Servicing Peripherals.* A continuation built on the foundations learned in the Fundamentals course. This self-paced, seven-unit instruction set acquaints the student with each category of peripheral devices, including printers, displays, disk drives, and modems. Through a combination of text and experiments the student will study the purpose, capabilities, and fundamentals of each peripheral and how each is interfaced to a mini or microcomputer. This course also covers the ETA standards for communications and nonstandard communications interfaces. Successful completion of this course earns 2.0 CEUs.

Course Outline

Unit 1. Communication Standards
Serial Communication
  Serial Fundamentals
  Advantages of Serial Communications
  Growth of Serial Communications
EIA Recommended Standards
  The First Standard
  Other EIA Standards
  The RS-232-C Standard
  RS-232-C Signal Definitions
  RS-232-C Signal Characteristics
  RS-232-C Mechanical Interface
  RS-232-C Interfacing Problems

Parallel Data Communications
  Parallel Fundamentals
  The IEEE Standard 488-1978 Interface
Other Interfaces
  Current Loop Interfaces
  Series Bus Interfaces
  The Centronics Parallel Interface

Unit 2. Input Peripherals
Keyboard Mechanics
  Keyboard Codes
  Types of Key Switches
  Key Switch Characteristics
  Key Roll-Over and Lock Out
Keyboard Electronics
  A Hexadecimal Keyboard
  An Alphanumeric Keyboard
  A Microprocessor-Encoded Keyboard
Alternative Input Devices
  Physical Input Devices
  Code Readers
  Badge Card Readers
Speech Recognition
  Types of Speech Recognition Devices
  Principles of Operation
  Typical Recognition System
  Interfacing a Voice System
Optical Readers
  Available Systems
  Optical Sensor Fundamentals
  Bar Code Readers
  OCR Readers

Unit 3. Visual Displays
Visual Display Fundamentals
  Cathode Ray Tube Operation
  The Phosphor Coating
  CRT Image Distortion

Stroke-Writing Displays
  Fundamentals
  Types of Systems
Raster Generation
  Raster Systems
  Image Presentation
  The Raster Process
  Raster Generating Signals
  Character Matrices
  Display Resolution
  Display Bandwidth
Color Displays
  Color CRTs
  Color CRT Fundamentals
  High Resolution Color
  Color Convergence
  CRT Monitors
Flat Panel Visual Displays
  Flat Panel Displays—Pros and Cons
  Segmented Displays
  Dot-Matrix Displays
  Types of Flat Panel Displays
  Plasma Displays
Liquid-Crystal Displays
  Types of LCDs
  Modes of Operation
  Display Interfacing
  Fonts

Unit 4. Printers and Plotters
Dot-Matrix Impact Printers
  Printing with Dots
  Character At-a-Time Printing
  Line At-a-Time Printing
  Character Generation
  Matrix Storage
  Paper-Feed Mechanisms

Solid-State Memory Peripherals
  Memory Emulators
  Disk Drive Emulators
  External Device Emulators and Printer Spoolers

Unit 6. Data Communications
Fundamentals of Data Communications
  Typical Data Communications Systems
  Standards in Data Communications
  Modes of Transmission
Modulation Techniques
  Complex Waves
  Amplitude Signaling Techniques
  FM and Phase Signaling Techniques
Wire Communications
  Data Lines and Modems

Unit 7. Peripherals in Computer Control Systems
Digital-to-Analog Converters
  The Adder Ladder
  An Example DAC Chip
  Applications
Analog-to-Digital Converters
  Simultaneous Conversion
  Continuous Conversion
  Elementary A to D Converter
  Successive Approximation
Digital Sensors and I/O Devices
  Input Devices
  Output Devices
Requires the disk drive upgrade for the ET-100 Advanced Microcomputer Trainer.

EC-2003 *Computer Servicing Maintenance.* This twenty-one-unit, self-paced course takes all of the knowledge gained from the basic and advanced courses taken to date and applies it to the techniques of troubleshooting both digital and microprocessor systems. The course briefly reviews some of the devices and then proceeds to exercises designed to make the student comfortable and proficient in standard digital troubleshooting techniques. Sections include the interaction one part of a computer has with others, using block diagrams to isolate problems, and learning to write system diagnostic programs for a particular system. Successful completion of this course earns 3.0 CEUs. You will not need any additional supplies.

Course Outline

Unit 1. Electrical Characteristics of TTL and MOS Devices
Voltage Parameters
   Data Sheets and Static Electrical Parameters
   Logic 1 and Logic 0 Input Voltages
   Input Diode Clamp Voltage
   Logic 1 and Logic 2 Output Voltages
   Notes on V_{IH}, V_{IL}, V_{OH} and V_{OL}
Current Parameters
   Logic 1 and Logic 0 Input Current
   Calculation of Fanout
   Output Short Circuit Current
MOS Static Electrical Parameters
Other Parameters
   Tristate Devices
   Open Collector Devices
   Digital Inputs and Outputs
   LSTTL Devices

Unit 2. Using a Logic Clip, Logic Probe, Pulser Probe, and
       Current Probe
Logic Level Testing
   The Logic Probe
   Logic Probe Summary
   The Logic Clip
Other Probes
   The Current Probe
   The Pulser Probe

Troubleshooting the Keyboard Circuits
Summary of Keyboard Checks

Unit 12. Signature Analysis
Introduction to Signature Analysis
The Problem
The Solution
Compressing a Bit Stream
A Practical Solution
Using Signature Analysis
Realities of Signature Analysis
Using Signature Analyzers
Analyzing Signatures

Unit 13. Troubleshooting the Printer Interface
Printer Connections
The Parallel Connection
Parallel Connection Summary
The Serial Connection
Summary of Parallel Communication
Parallel Printer Interfacing
An Actual Printer Interface
Initializing the Printer and Computer
Printer Troubleshooting
Getting Started
A System Loop

Unit 14. Troubleshooting Display Circuits
Video Displays
Video Output Devices
The Sync and Video Signals
Composite Video Signal
Character Generation
Single Character Generation
Character Generator ROM
Displaying a Character
Scanning the Rows

CRT Preventive Maintenance
Keyboard Preventive Maintenance

Unit 20. Constructing Your Own Troubleshooting Aids
The Static Stimulus Tester
   Address Stimulus
   Data Receive + Data Display
   Address Line Display
   Asynchronous Input Receive + Display
   Control Bit Stimulus
   SST Summary
LSA Substitutes
   Address Catcher
   Address Catcher Hardware
   Using the Address Catcher
   Mobile I/O Port
   Outputting Data on the Fly
Controlling ROM-Based Diagnostics
   Mobile I/O Port Construction

Unit 21. Tools and Equipment
Hand Tools including: Screwdrivers, Pliers, Wirecutters, Wire Strippers, and Wrenches.
Soldering and Desoldering Tools
Care and Handling of Tools
Test Equipment including: Logic Clip, Logic Probe, Pulser Probe and Current Probe. Section also reviews other test equipment already covered.

ADVANCED MICROPROCESSOR SELF-STUDY COURSE

The following self-directed course material is courtesy of Heath Company, Benton Harbor, Michigan.

EE-8088 *Advanced Microprocessors.* This ten-unit self-paced course taken in conjunction with the ET-100 Computer Trainer is a comprehensive course designed to make the student fully knowledgeable in sixteen-bit microprocessor technology. The package includes more than 200 pages of software programming and interfacing experiments to accompany 1,200 pages of text. This course would be the logical step after completing the Computer Servicing Series to enhance your knowledge of the most up-to-date computer systems. Successful completion of the course earns eight CEUs. The current cost of the course is $99.95 plus shipping. Requires the ET-100 Computer Trainer.

Course Objectives.

When the student completes the course he or she should be able to do the following:

1. Describe the internal structure of a typical microprocessor.
2. Design a simple microcomputer.
3. Interface a microprocessor to the outside world.
4. Write programs using Assembly language.

Course Outline

Unit Number	Description
1	Microcomputer Basics
2	Introduction to Programming
3	Expanded Programming
4	Expanded Addressing and the Programming Instruction Set
5	Memory Segmentation
6	Data Handling
7	Interfacing Part 1
8	Interfacing Part 2
9	Software Programming
10	Hardware Interfacing
Appendix A	Number Systems Data
Appendix B	Machine Coding Instructions
Appendix C	Computer Arithmetic
Appendix D	Instruction Set
Appendix E	Data Sheets

NOTE: Each of the ten sections has a series of experiments to reinforce the text materials.

SUMMARY

It's quite obvious that a wealth of information, knowledge, and training can be yours using self-directed educational courses. However, the same caution exists here as it did for correspondence or home study. You must have the self-discipline to stick to a schedule and apply yourself. Earlier, a cost comparison between all of the previously stated educational options and the self-directed educational courses was mentioned. To that end, let's look at the current costs for each of these educational units and at the cost of the required accessories.

Self-Directed Materials Cost

Course Identification	Cost
EI-3133 Soldering Course	$ 29.95
EE-3101 -B DC Electronics	$ 99.95
EE-3102-B AC Electronics	$ 99.95
EE-3103-B Semiconductor Devices	$ 99.95
EE-3104-B Electronic Circuits	$ 99.95
EE-3201-A Digital Techniques	$149.95
Total Text Costs (plus shipping)	$ 579.70

Additional Equipment, Training Materials, Tools

ET-3600 Analog Trainer	$ 149.95
SM-2380 Multimeter	$ 89.95
S0-4552 Oscilloscope	$ 419.95
ET-3700 Digital Trainer	$ 149.95
GHP-1270 Hand Tools/Soldering Iron	$ 59.95
Basic Cassette Recorder (estimate)	$ 30.00
Subtotal of Equipment & Supplies:	$ 899.75
+ Instructional Text	$ 579.70
Total Cost:	$1,479.45

The total cost compares favorably with other methods of non-degree granting courses and allows you to proceed at your own pace, allocating funds for equipment that will be of use to you in your career as you are able. Regardless of the approach you decide to take, remember that an education is an investment in your future.

FOR MORE INFORMATION

For more information about Heath Continuing Education Products write:

Heath Company
   Benton Harbor, MI 49022

CHAPTER 7

WHERE THE JOBS ARE

Perhaps no other field has touched and influenced our lives as much as the field of high technology. The development of computers has created a wide range of job opportunities that did not exist fifty years ago, including careers in computer maintenance. This chapter will identify and define those areas where employment opportunities for computer maintenance specialists abound.

WHAT IS COMPUTER MAINTENANCE?

A computer maintenance technician is a specially trained electronics technician whose job encompasses all forms of repairs, installations, and modifications to computers and computer-controlled systems. Computer maintenance technicians may work in a factory or repair facility, or they may be assigned to specific customers. Duties include routine adjustments and service (preventive maintenance), diagnosing specific problems (failures) at the customer's business or at a repair facility, and making repairs, installing new or additional equipment, or performing similar duties at a manufacturing facility. As with most career fields, employment opportunities in computer maintenance can be grouped into several categories, and each of the categories can be examined to see how many opportunities exist within it. The major categories of employment for computer maintenance specialists are the government, private industry, and the service industry.

JOBS WITH THE GOVERNMENT

The government can be divided into two components. The first is the military service and the second includes the civilian employees within the government. The military is defined as the Department of Defense and its subdivisions—the Army, Navy, Air Force, Marine Corps, and Coast Guard. Of course, some overlap occurs within each of these categories. The military has civilian employees as well as service personnel, so the distinction must therefore be made between service personnel and Department of Defense civilians. Service personnel are men and women who have joined or enlisted in their respective branches of the service for anywhere from two to six years and are trained in specific jobs called military occupational specialties. These jobs range from purely military-related fields to specialized areas of high technology. These people receive specialized training and are paid while they learn. They may be classified as either commissioned or noncommissioned officers.

Department of Defense civilians may work for any of the individual services, or they may be employees of the Department of Defense without a specific service affiliation. These men and women are usually already skilled in their individual fields and are classified as civil service employees. Again, like their military counterparts, they may be involved in many different fields, from clerical to high technology. Like all government employees, they are rated or ranked according to a government service rating number (GS) that establishes their level of competency as well as pay scale. In some cases, the civilian employees of the major services will be assigned to duties at military installations outside of the United States. Many of the civilian employees come from the ranks of active-duty service personnel either on completion of their enlistments or on retirement. The civilian component of the military adds a stability, especially to the high-technology field, that is not easily obtained with service personnel.

Two Army Profiles

Sgt. Margret Soyars is an instructor assigned to the army's Computer Maintenance School at Fort Gordon, Georgia. Enlisting first in the reserves, she completed her educational requirements for a high school diploma and was initially trained as a wheeled vehicle/power generator mechanic. After serving nearly four years in the service, Margret found that she was limited in the types of repairs she could do and was "tired of feeling dirty and grubby." So she reenlisted as a 39B computer maintenance specialist and was sent to Fort Gordon, Georgia, for training. As a sergeant, she was also eligible for supervisory training and completed nearly a full year of training with an interruption for the birth of a child.

Sgt. Soyars became permanent party—that is, she was assigned directly to a military school instead of being made a temporarily assigned student—and was able after the birth of her child to complete the final phase of training. The final phase of instruction, a practical exercise, required the student to connect the external power cables from the generator system to the completely equipped mobile repair facility. The cables weighed in excess of fifty pounds and had to be lifted upward and into a connector. For the first time in her army experience, Sgt. Soyars found her activities restricted, not because of her sex, but rather because of her pregnancy. Shortly after her baby was born, she rejoined her class, performed the final phase of her course, and was picked to become one of several female instructors at the 39B Computer Maintenance School. Her duties include hands-on training of students, preparing lesson plans, and supervising classroom activities. She also serves as a senior source of technical expertise in her given field. Sgt. Soyars is qualified to instruct or supervise personnel who operate a mobile repair facility. The mission of such a facility is to provide immediate repair support for the highly complex computer systems and control circuitry on the army's newest helicopter, the Apache, which one senior civilian instructor described as a flying platform for computers. Sgt. Soyars is accepted as a technical specialist and noncommissioned officer first, and as a woman, wife, and mother second.

As a sergeant (E-5) with over five years of service, Margret earns approximately $22,152 a year. This figure includes the taxable salary component of $13,296 with the balance of $8,856 consisting of tax-exempt allowances. Her salary compares with many civilian positions, but Sgt. Soyars, as a member of the army, also receives free medical care for herself and family as well as educational benefits, a retirement plan, and up to thirty days vacation yearly. She is constantly taking advantage of educational opportunities available to her to further her career growth.

Debbie is a Department of the Army civilian assigned to the Army Signal Corps, Fort Monmouth, New Jersey. After completing her high school education, she enlisted in the air force and was trained as an avionics (aircraft electronics) specialist. Debbie was assigned to an air force base where she progressed from basic avionics maintenance to advanced techniques. She continued to further her education by on-the-job training as she learned how to maintain the complex combination of electronics, microprocessors, and control circuitry that make up a modern military airplane. During her tour of duty, Debbie also furthered her education by taking community college courses and correspondence courses that were offered through and paid by the air force. Finally, on completion of her military tour of duty, which coincided with graduation from the Cleveland Institute of Electronics Home Study Course in Microprocessor Technology, she applied for a civil service job with the Department of the Army.

The Department of the Army sent Debbie to advanced training schools and seminars and assigned her as a technical representative for a specialized tactical computer system. Her job takes her to posts throughout the United States and overseas. As a Department of the Army civilian, Debbie has a GS-09 rating, which provides a salary in excess of $25,000 a year, an excellent retirement and benefit program, and opportunities for advancement and education, not to mention travel. On the job, Debbie serves as a senior source of technical expertise for the tactical computer and trains military and civilian personnel in its use. Periodically, she oversees enhancements, modifications, or renovations to the computer and is sometimes called upon to submit detailed technical reports on the effects of these modifications on the system's ability to perform its mission.

In her free time, Debbie continues her education by studying computer languages. This effort is directed at enhancing her ability to solve problems and qualifying her for career advancement within her specialty field.

Other Government Employees

The federal government is our country's largest single employer. The list of government agencies and departments would fill several books this size and probably still not cover all of them. Each agency and department recruits personnel for available positions, tests candidates, and assigns successful ones a civil service status and a GS rating for pay purposes. With the rapid growth of high technology, the government is increasingly becoming a major source of jobs within the computer maintenance field. Such departments and agencies as the Department of State, Central Intelligence Agency, Department of Labor, and Postal Service all need and recruit computer maintenance personnel.

JOBS IN PRIVATE INDUSTRY

The private industry side of the career field can also be divided into many categories. Simply defined, private industry is the private sector where a product is designed, engineered, and built for resale to others. As this simple definition suggests, private industry offers opportunities in design, engineering, production, manufacturing, quality control, and service, to mention just a few. Each of these areas has numerous divisions within its overall title. Another area, OEM (original equipment manufacturer), should be given particular consideration. Much, if not all, consumer electronics equipment is made by a handful of companies. For example, although there are probably a dozen or more brands of videocassette recorders (each recorder with at least one microprocessor), no more than five firms are responsible for their manufacture. These companies are called OEMs, and they sell a product to another company to relabel and market. This practice is quite common in the automobile industry as well.

Among the numerous career opportunities available in the private sector for computer maintenance specialists are those in data processing, biomedical/medical devices, consumer electronics, automotive electronics/control, industrial process and control, test equipment and automated testing technology, aircraft (avionics systems), and communications. In private industry, employees usually come to a company with some background in the field and are trained to perform specific tasks on that industry or company's product line. Salaries may be based on hourly rates or may be part of a weekly, monthly, or yearly compensation package.

Research and Design

Before any product can be sold, it must evolve. Engineers and computer maintenance specialists often prepare drawings and specifications and build prototypes from a concept or proposal. A prototype is a representation of what the final product should be, in most cases, minus the fancy case and the frills. Computer maintenance specialists who are skilled electronics technicians work side by side with the design engineers, translating concepts and drawings to the actual product. Computer maintenance specialists within the R&D (research and development) environment are usually more senior personnel who have a variety of skills, including a good knowledge of both hardware and software. Hardware can be defined as the physical parts that would make up a computer system, such as the chips, circuits, and drives. Software, on the other hand, consists of instructions to the microprocessor or computer written by programmers to facilitate the overall operation of the computer. Some of these instructions are actually placed permanently on microchips called ROMs. These are read-only memory chips that contain the information needed to start up the computer and perform certain housekeeping and traffic-management tasks. Other software, available on diskette or tape, contains the operating system—that is, the actual instructions that transform a collection of components into a viable and productive computing device. Software present on ROM chips is frequently referred to as firmware, because the contents cannot be easily altered. The instructions have been "burned" into an integrated circuit, whereas diskette-based software can readily be changed.

Maintenance specialists assigned to work with the engineering team typically have three to five years of experience in the field together with such skills as drafting ability, mechanical skills, software/firmware skills, and, of course, those skills usually associated with computer maintenance personnel. They may be involved in the actual engineering process, making prototype circuit boards, assembling and testing circuits, and ensuring that the engineer's concepts become real circuitry. Another duty is debugging. This term is common to the computer world and simply means finding out why something didn't work the way it was supposed to. Debugging, especially debugging prototype circuits, accounts for a good deal of a computer maintenance specialist's time—especially in the R&D environment.

AN R & D PROFILE

Jeff is a senior computer maintenance specialist who works in the R&D section of a leading supplier of microcomputers. After high school, Jeff attended a junior college and obtained his associate degree in electronics technology. He then settled into an entry-level position with his present employer. As a junior or entry-level technician, Jeff was exposed to the entire range of maintenance tasks, from simply replacing components on circuit boards to identifying and replacing defective system components. Taking advantage of company-sponsored educational opportunities, Jeff progressed from an entry-level position to that of senior maintenance specialist in about eighteen months. At this time, an opening was available on his company's research and development team, and Jeff's skills and willingness to learn earned him the assignment.

Jeff is now assigned to work with the senior software and hardware design engineers in developing business computer systems for their company's clients. Jeff's duties vary from one day to the next. One day he might be involved in making special test fixtures to allow prototype components to interact. Another day might be software/ firmware-oriented where he actually is involved in transferring the coded instructions onto ROM chips for use in the company's latest computer. Yet another day might bring the need to talk with prospective suppliers of components, with Jeff serving as the interface between a manufacturer's representative and his company to ensure that his firm's specifications are met by the manufacturer's representative or vendor. According to Jeff, the job never gets boring, with new challenges on a daily basis. He can move easily within the R&D environment, drafting a circuit, writing reports, or physically making circuits. Additionally,

Jeff handles some telephone inquiries from the field, either from the sales staff or directly from customers with specific questions or problems with their computers. Being a senior level specialist, he is able to function with minimal supervision. Jeff is familiar with the systems, how they were built, and what they can do, and he is perhaps the best-qualified person to advise a customer on their specific application. Jeff's salary reflects his experience, skill, and willingness to continue his education. As a senior specialist, he earns in excess of $35,000 per year plus all of the benefits usually associated with working for a large corporation. As to the future, Jeff is attending night school and hopes to earn his engineering degree and thereby grow even more with his company.

Manufacturing

Once a product has been developed, it must be mass-produced. Production or manufacturing of computers and computer-related products requires a growing number of computer maintenance personnel.

The role of the computer maintenance specialist can begin even before the product is manufactured. Incoming inspection, quality assurance, and quality control are some of the areas where computer maintenance specialists can find themselves. All of these titles are basically related to one fact—ensuring that the components and parts supplied by a variety of vendors meet the company's standards for quality and reliability. Incoming inspection specialists operate a variety of complex test equipment to ensure that a given component operates and meets stated specifications. A technician involved in this area must be able to read specifications and blueprints and must know how to operate a diverse assortment of test equipment. This incoming inspection can either make or break a product's reputation for reliability. If the individual components that make up a system are faulty or irregular, then the final system will probably not be reliable. Conversely, if the incoming materials meet or exceed specifications, then the final product will be more apt to be reliable.

It's usually more practical to let machines assist in the assembly of computer systems. As discussed earlier, N/C (numerically controlled) machines are capable of performing much of the work usually done by a human being. In the case of the computer, another computer actually helps in their manufacture. An N/C component insertion machine can place the separate components into the correct holes on circuit boards, perform simple testing, and then permanently make the connections via a device called a wave soldering machine. An example of this computer-building-a-computer technology is at IBM's highly automated facility in the Southeast, where portable laptop computers are assembled by machine at the rate of several computers per minute. However, errors by either human beings or machines do exist, and computer maintenance specialists are needed to resolve these problems on the assembly line. Computer maintenance specialists may be involved in a testing situation where a product is subjected to specific tests to ensure reliability prior to going further along in the cycle, or they may be involved in a final test at the end of the production cycle. Regardless, the role of the computer maintenance technician will be to identify and resolve any problems found in the equipment. Once the equipment has passed through the final test, it should be reliable and ready for shipment to the customer.

However, the very nature and flexibility of the personal or small desktop microcomputer allow for customizing or tailoring it to meet a specific requirement. Computer maintenance specialists involved in this area are called configuration specialists. A configuration specialist takes a sales order specifying exactly what options or accessories are to be supplied and installed in a specific computer and then accomplishes the installation and testing.

Computers are a lot like cars. You can buy them fully equipped or you can buy them stripped. The essential desktop computer consists of the computer proper and a keyboard. Accessories include disk drives, video display cards, and monitors. The configuration specialist examines a customer's order and then installs the accessories. In addition, this technical specialist performs specialized tests to ensure that all of the equipment is operational and works together as specified. The configuration technician's role requires mechanical as well as electronics skills. He or she may be called upon to physically install combinations of mechanical and electronic devices, fashion specialized cables, and modify existing cabinets to accommodate the additional components. Upon completion of the installation of all accessories, the configuration technician is also responsible for the predelivery final test, which consists of an operational test of the entire computer system over a period of days to ensure that no problems will occur.

JOBS IN THE SERVICE INDUSTRY

For every computer or computer-controlled device sold, there must be someone somewhere able to repair it. The service segment of the industry provides this capability in three distinct levels. These levels are the manufacturer's own service department, third-party service organizations, and independent service specialists. No matter what the title or organizational affiliation, the task remains the same—to provide service to a customer. Recently, a study conducted for the International Association of Field Service Managers revealed that four of the major computer manufacturers reported that service revenue, that is to say, the moneys generated as a result of service activities and not sales, accounted for nearly 20 percent of their total yearly revenue. This does not take into account the additional sales revenues generated as a result of a firm having a good customer service organization.

Service industry personnel are known by many different titles. The one thing they all share is their overall mission of customer satisfaction and support. Many companies have formally acknowledged the fact that a service specialist is an extension of the corporate image by referring to them as customer service engineers rather than as computer maintenance technicians or simply service personnel. The reason for this becomes fairly obvious if you consider that more than eighty companies produce a similar desktop computer system, the IBM-PC or PC-compatible. Each company subscribes to the standards in design, form, and function as set down by the original product produced by IBM. A customer's decision to buy a product can be influenced either positively or negatively by the availability of service. Even though technology has advanced, a device as complex as a computer will eventually require service. The customer, prior to purchase, must be assured that this service and support will be available and in particular, that service personnel will be available to meet their requirements on a timely and cost-effective basis.

Naturally, a customer purchasing a computer system from, for example, IBM, will not be concerned about the availability of service. IBM is one of the firms that operates its own factory service operation. An IBM account or service representative will be assigned to the customer and be responsible for installation of the equipment as well as any after-sales service support required during the warranty period. Later, the customer can elect to purchase a service agreement and thereby be assured that all service requirements are met for a fixed yearly fee. Other large manufacturers have similar, in-house service organizations. Smaller companies elect to farm out, or contract, their service requirements to third-party service organizations or independent service specialists.

Regardless of the method in which service will be accomplished, the end result, customer satisfaction and support, is of the utmost importance.

The Manufacturer's Own Service Organization

Usually only larger, older firms have their own service organization. Service centers are positioned throughout the country in areas of greatest customer density and are staffed by factory-trained personnel who specialize only in the equipment sold by their respective companies. Service can be provided on a carry-in basis or at the customer's place of business. Service specialists involved in the manufacturer's service organization are referred to as field service engineers, customer service engineers, customer service representatives, product support specialists, or service engineers. Rarely will a company refer to its service staff as technicians. Staffers come to a company with a firm foundation in basic and advanced electronics, are trained in factory-sponsored schools on specific products, and then are assigned to field offices. They may be trained on only one product or on a family of products, and they provide service and support to products manufactured or supplied by their company. Factory-service organizations do not provide service to products from other than company-approved suppliers. The organization may service devices such as printers or monitors that were not made by their parent company if these devices were sold (supplied) as part of a customer's order.

Smaller companies may also have their own factory-service organizations. However, these groups tend to be local and not national in scope. If a manufacturer establishes an in-house service department, then all repairs to its equipment would be handled at the factory level. However, the customer would be responsible for returning a system requiring service to the factory for repairs. The system would then be checked, serviced, and reshipped to the customer. In order to spare the customer the inconvenience and lost time shipping a system back to a factory causes, many manufacturers have elected to authorize or contract the service to third-party service organizations.

Third-Party Service Organizations

Third-party service organizations are large national firms whose primary business is to provide service and support to a wide variety of products, as opposed to the manufacturer's service department, which will service only the firm's own product lines. Like the manufacturer's own service department, the third-party service organization can provide service and support on a local or regional basis.

Also like the manufacturer's own service staff, these third-party organizations are located in regions with a high concentration of customers for the products they have elected to support and service. The duties and job titles remain essentially the same, but the scope of service is expanded to encompass a wider variety of products and manufacturers. Third-party service allows customers to contract for all of their computer service and support requirements regardless of the original equipment supplier. Some third-party service organizations provide warranty service for a manufacturer and in effect serve as an authorized extension of that given supplier. In this case, the firm may list itself as an authorized service center for products manufactured by that firm. Service can be provided at the service center level or at the customer's site, and contracts ensuring service on all equipment for a fixed yearly rate are likewise available.

Service personnel at a third-party service center are trained on a variety of equipment, not just on a single product or product line. The same service specialist who installs a laser printer may also service the customer's facsimile machine, despite the fact that they have been supplied by different companies. The third-party service organization provides a much broader variety of services to a customer and can provide them in areas where factory service is either not available or impractical. No matter what product is supported or who the manufacturer is, the end goal of a third-party service organization is to provide customer support and service. Third-party service allows even the smallest computer manufacturer to offer local or regional service to its clients on a cost-effective basis.

On-site Service Specialists

Private industry has rapidly and completely embraced the personal computer. In fact, many industries have converted from large centralized information management facilities to local personal computers on desks linked by a network of cables to a central, larger personal computer called a server. This permits people to access and manipulate, and more important, share information either within an office or, in many cases, throughout the country. The insurance and legal professions are massive consumers of personal computers and computing, and because of the proliferation of these systems, these organizations can justify the cost of having their own personal system specialists on staff.

This is a relatively new opportunity for employment and one that differs from those we've explored in this chapter. The on-site or personal service specialist is not only the maintenance technician, but many times is also the installer and system administrator for his or her employer. In addition to excellent technical skills, the specialist must be familiar with both the hardware and software used by the employer. It is not enough to be technically competent; the on-site or captive service specialist must be able to install and then teach or assist the end user in the best ways of using the technology. This is where interpersonal skills and communication really come to bear. Not everyone can handle the daily interaction with people. Most technicians and engineers for that matter are more comfortable interacting and interfacing with technology. What makes them good at that aspect of their job frequently makes them less than adequate when it comes to one-on-one interactions.

The on-site service specialist must be adept at explaining technology to people who have never had the opportunity to exploit it. They must be capable of alleviating fears that this new piece of equipment will replace the employees or cause them to lose their jobs. The proliferation of software requires that specialists be as adept at using different word processors as they are at configuring systems. The two are permanently interlinked—joined at the technical equivalent of "the hip."

A private business or industry looks at computers as adjuncts to productivity, and as such they expect the computer to function with little or no downtime or problems. If a system fails, they obviously expect their own service specialist to be able to resolve the problem in record time. Management is not so much interested in why or how a given piece of technology failed, but rather how soon it can be returned to productive service.

The on-site specialist also may be responsible for operating the help-desk. Although the function does not require physically sitting at a desk, the job does require that the specialist be able to rapidly trace a problem to its source and then resolve the problem. This might require a physical visit to the desk where the employee reported the problem, or it could be accomplished remotely, either by accessing the employee's computer or by being able to talk the person through the problem.

Not all problems will be technical or hardware related. The average problem, according to our industry sources, might very well be users not understanding what they are expected to do next. An example of this sort of problem was reported by a major manufacturer of personal computers. Their help-desk received dozens of similar calls from new computer users. These calls all had one thing in common: the caller was asking where the "Any Key" was located on their computer keyboard. It seems that one particular software program had a screen message instructing the user to "Press any key to continue," and the new computer users could not find this key!

Like it or not, the on-site service specialist will probably deal more with problems of this nature than with technically challenging ones, but the result is the same. If the computer is not operating, the user can not accomplish his or her job, and someone has to fix it!

Salary and benefit packages for an on-site service specialist compare favorably with other service positions and might very well include additional opportunities for advancement and continuing education.

Service specialists can *never* stop learning, unless of course they want to stop *earning!*

Independent Service Specialists

This last category accounts for a great deal of local, personalized service. If a small customer base exists in a given area, and third-party or manufacturer's service organizations are not available, then the customer logically turns to the independent service specialist. An independent service specialist is exactly what the title states, a businessperson engaged in the service industry. The independent service specialist is like your local television repair shop in that it is independent of any manufacturer's affiliation, provides local limited service, and is probably run by one or two people.

The independent service specialist operates in a restricted area, usually in a small town or city, and provides a variety of technical support and service to customers on a wide range of equipment. Usually this support and service is provided when factory or third-party service is not available, but there are exceptions. Many independent service specialists have established themselves in areas that already have both manufacturers and third-party service by offering more support or personalized services at lower costs. Their technical staff may be smaller and more limited, and the service facilities may be smaller, but to a number of customers their local nature makes them a plus. Independent service specialists are also found at or employed by local computer stores. In this case, the specialists are employees of the individual stores and service and support the equipment their store sells. Like other service specialists, they attend factory/manufacturer sponsored seminars to learn the latest techniques in servicing equipment. Some independent service specialists also contract their services to local governmental entities, including schools, to provide a variety and level of service most likely to meet their client's needs and budget. In some isolated cases, independent service specialists serve as a manufacturer's authorized service center for an area too small to make direct or third-party service practical. Again, the goal of the independent service specialist is to provide service and support to a customer base.

Regardless of where you seek employment, a career in computer maintenance is closely tied to good customer relations, service, and support. Good service and support make for customer satisfaction. The growth of the computer and high-technology fields has opened up opportunities that did not exist when you started your education. More and more people and businesses are making use of and exploiting this high technology, assuring you of continued employment and growth regardless of where you live.

ADVANCEMENT IN THE FIELD

Unlike many careers, computer maintenance is the gateway to bigger and better employment opportunities. Many industry representatives, as well as the U.S. Department of Labor, paint a very rosy picture for the person selecting a career in computer maintenance. Service personnel have a unique opportunity to see both sides of an operation. As employees of a company, government agency, or service center, they are technically competent and skilled problem solvers. As the interface and the people most likely to interact with the customer, they gain unique insights into problems, applications, and human relations. It is for this very reason that many companies promote service personnel into sales and other marketing-related duties. Such individuals have proven themselves competent to be company representatives by virtue of both their technical expertise and their customer-relations skills. It has been said that "when it comes down to the bare facts, all things are pretty much the same, people buy from people they like." Translated into context, this phrase can be applied to the fact that many companies produce computers and that from a technical standpoint, these computers are all, with few exceptions, the same. A customer is therefore more likely to choose one computer over another because he or she feels comfortable with the person selling it.

This doesn't mean that a company's reputation, product line, cost-effectiveness, and other factors won't enter into the decision-making process. They will, but the bottom line is that people buy products from people they like. A computer maintenance specialist is the most visible member of his or her organization in terms of the customer. The sales specialist comes in, makes a presentation, gets an order, and will probably not see the customer again until it's time for another order. On the other hand, the computer maintenance specialist will be on the customer's site for a preinstallation survey, will return to install the equipment and possibly help train the staff, and will be physically present when service is required. Perhaps that's why Dwight Johnson, national field service manager for Abbott Medical, has said, "Give me a person who is 35 percent technical and 65 percent public relations. The equipment isn't all that hard to learn, but good customer relations and PR are worth their weight in gold." Abbott, like many other companies, looks to the ranks of its field service organization when marketing positions open up. Like many others, it believes that the service engineer understands his or her product and company and has already established a good working relationship with the client.

If sales isn't your cup of tea, perhaps being a technical trainer will be more to your liking. Technical trainers provide the customer with instruction on both the hardware and software purchased. These skilled individuals are usually assigned to a given customer or client when the equipment has been delivered and installed, and they conduct classroom training on how to operate both the computers and software. They may conduct these classes informally, on a one-to-one basis, or in a formalized classroom setting. Trainers frequently come from the ranks of service specialists who are intimately familiar with the equipment and are further schooled in instructional and classroom presentation techniques. As noted earlier, the more you learn about computers, technology, and programming languages, the more you can expect to earn. The entire high-technology industry is in a constant state of change with new developments occurring on a regular basis. Likewise, enhancements, improvements, and new technologies are emerging at about the same pace. What this means is that if your skills were learned seven years ago and you haven't been involved in continuing education, you stand a good chance of being "obsoleted" by new technology.

Assuming that sales or technical training doesn't appeal to you, there are still many other fields available that will provide upward mobility. All they require is building on the foundation established when you became a computer maintenance specialist.

PC/microprocessor programmers and analysts perform detailed program design, coding, testing, documentation, and implementation of real-time or interactive systems. They may use interconnected or networked computer systems. Program designing may consist of application modules or specific programs to support such subfunctions as communications and signal-processing graphic controls. Trends show an increased need for programmers and analysts whose skills are such that they can produce the necessary applications software to interface the personal or desktop computer with the large mainframe system. Most opportunities require at least one year of experience with one of the more high-level structured languages, such as COBOL or FORTRAN.

Systems (software/firmware) programmers create and maintain operating systems, communications, database, and other applications software. Within a given company they might also be responsible for the support and modifications made to existing software applications, provide planning and technical expertise, evaluate and modify existing systems, or create entirely new special-purpose software. Programmers may also find themselves responsible for documentation and training. Strong demand is expected to continue across a broad front, including manufacturing, computer service organizations, and management and consulting firms. Opportunities are opening in the field of artificial intelligence, which involves programming a computer to react to a set series of problems in much the same way a human specialist might. Educational requirements usually include a bachelor's degree in computer science as well as direct exposure to interfacing and computer systems and software.

Technical writers/editors are responsible for the production of a variety of documents and publications, ranging from proposals to end-user manuals. They must have a firm understanding of the technology as well as the ability to express this knowledge in a clear and concise manner. The position also requires the ability to interface and interact with technical specialists and with client personnel. Principal responsibilities can extend beyond the realm of technical communications to marketing and sales support in both a written or audiovisual format. Employment outlook is such that the demand for quality writers and editors far exceeds the supply. Positions increasingly require knowledge of sophisticated publication techniques as well as a firm technical knowledge. A background in marketing and writing is an asset as is a degree in computer science, technical communications, or journalism.

Senior analysts, project leaders, and consultants are typically responsible for liaison with the end user, system specification, design, and project control. They may also act as supervisors of other analysts, programmers, and support personnel, providing implementation and programming. They are the key link between the computing resources and the end-users. Consultants function as senior, highly skilled, and specialized resources to both industry and the end user. Their skills in a given discipline enable them to provide advice, counsel, and expert information on a variety of problems and applications. Their services are frequently made available on a contract to a given customer, enabling the consultant to function as an independent professional in much the same manner as a doctor or lawyer. Consultants also provide customers with the expertise not readily available within their corporate environment, and further, this expertise is purchased for the period required, freeing up capital for other purposes. Industry forecasts show a trend toward the use of consultants where a specific problem must be addressed in a relatively short time frame. The very nature of the consultant allows a task to be completed by a highly skilled, versatile individual whose expertise is the product of a combination of education and experience. The minimum educational requirement for these positions is a bachelor's degree in computer science. For consultant assignments, an M.B.A. degree is preferred together with extensive exposure to computer science and the business community.

Managers are developed from the ranks of those already employed in a given field. In the high-technology, computer maintenance field, the person having a combination of above average technical skills coupled with a firm foundation in interpersonal relationships has the best chance for advancement to management. Trends show an increase in management positions corresponding to the overall growth of the field. The best managers are those who can motivate people to work *with* them rather than *for* them. Additional education beyond the level required for the position is also a key ingredient leading to promotion to a managerial or supervisory position.

Mobility Profile

Perhaps Ron best illustrates just how far one can progress in the field from a beginning as a computer maintenance specialist. In 1976 Ron, a recent college graduate, assumed a position as a field service engineer for a company producing desktop computers for the business community. Up until the late 1970s, computers were still large and usually only affordable by larger corporations. However, Ron had the opportunity to join a new firm whose product line was designed and priced with the average business user in mind.

Ron worked his territory, building good customer relations, installing equipment, handling service calls, and resolving problems. In fact, he became so good at interaction with customers that he was promoted to the sales and marketing department. Once in a marketing environment, Ron used the skills he'd developed as a field service engineer and his one-on-one understanding of a customer's needs and concerns to become one of the best sales representatives his company had. Hard work and excellent results accounted for Ron's further promotion, this time to director of marketing, where he again used the client knowledge and communication skills he'd learned in the field to earn his company an excellent reputation as a leading supplier of desktop business computing systems.

Today Ron is still with the same firm. His position and responsibilities have grown, but he is still concerned with good customer relations, something he learned as a field service engineer. How far can you advance within the computer industry? It all depends. Starting as a field service engineer, Ron's only been able to work himself up to company president!

GROWTH RATE AND EARNINGS

According to the U.S. Labor Department statistics, approximately 69,249 computer service specialists held jobs in 1986. Projections show an 80.42 percent growth rate with some 124,941 positions to be occupied by the year 2000. The growth rate is said to be faster than average, and the entire computer field is considered the most explosive of all industries when employment opportunities are considered.

Equal opportunity is the rule and not the exception, with nearly 23 percent of all positions filled by women and minorities. If anything, the industry as a whole is actively seeking out qualified women and minority applicants for positions and has an excellent record of providing training to ensure their eventual success.

Earnings, again according to Labor Department statistics, show that the median weekly earnings of full-time computer service technicians were about $514 per week, up from the $500 per week reported in 1984. The middle 50 percent earned between $409 and $660 per week, up from the 1984 figures of $375 and $625. The lowest 10 percent, considered entry or trainee level earned less than $304 per week, a figure again up from the 1984 report of $270. The highest 10 percent reported earnings of over $785 per week, up from $740 in 1984. The salary figures are based on a national average and do not reflect such benefits as a company car, expense account, medical and life insurance, and retirement benefits. A salary survey developed by geographical region is presented in Appendix A. It allows you to see salary ranges in various parts of the country.

HAVE YOU GOT WHAT IT TAKES?

You've now had the opportunity to gain some valuable information on this career field, but are you right for a career as a computer maintenance specialist? There's an easy way to find out. Listed below are some of the traits many service managers and personnel directors use to evaluate prospective employees. You can look over this list and rate yourself as outstanding, good, adequate, or poor. Obviously the more ratings in the outstanding or good category you have, the better. After you have rated yourself, give this list to someone who knows you and let that person rate you. There's no hard-and-fast guarantee that if you pass or fail a rating that you aren't right for a career in computer maintenance. Rather, look at this list as the guide to what your future boss will be looking for in a computer maintenance specialist.

1. *First Impression*—As the applicant impresses you, so is he or she likely to impress others. A person's first impression can set the pattern for future effectiveness.

2. *Physical Appearance*—Was the applicant well groomed and dressed in good taste? Keep in mind that he or she is trying to impress you favorably in putting the best foot forward.

3. *Voice and Speech*—Was the applicant's voice clear and easy to understand? Did you notice any annoying speech or voice habits?

4. *Educational Background*—Are the applicant's educational level and college/vo-technical grades acceptable? Is the applicant too well educated for the job?

5. *Poise and Self-Confidence*—Was the applicant at ease during the interview? Did the applicant seem to have a sound estimate of his or her abilities?

6. *Ambition*—What are the applicant's future goals? Are they realistic ones? Does the applicant seem motivated for the job and eager to succeed?

7. *Intelligence*—Does the applicant seem to grasp things easily? Is the applicant a good listener? Does the applicant ask thoughtful and intelligent questions?

8. *Knowledge of Our Company*—Did the applicant know anything about the company before the interview? Did he or she check with anyone about the company? Did the applicant have a good concept of the job itself?

9. *Maturity*—Does the applicant impress you as a person whose overall personality is suitable for the job? Does the applicant seem sufficiently mature in appearance and manner to deal effectively with the job?

10. *Overall Impression*—Is the applicant the kind of person you would like to have work with you? What is your overall, objective evaluation of this person—did the applicant "sell you?"

This profile is scored as follows: 3 points for every outstanding, 2 points for every good, 1 point for each adequate, and 0 for every poor. According to industry sources who use this type profile form, scores of 20 to 30 are considered very good to excellent; 15 to 19, average; 10 to 14, marginal; and anything below 10, poor. What is interesting, and something you should keep in mind, is the fact that only one question really dealt with technical competence; the others evaluate your ability to interact with others. If you didn't score as high as you hoped, at least you have some idea of what companies look for when they interview computer maintenance specialists. And you can always work to improve yourself.

CHAPTER 8

HOW TO GET A JOB

With your technical training behind you, you are now ready to become a member of the "real world" and find a job. Because of your extensive preparation, combined with the rapid growth of the career field you've prepared for, there shouldn't be any problem in finding a job. Remember, according to the Labor Department's figures, the computer maintenance and computer-related employment outlook is showing a growth rate far above normal, with a figure in excess of 80 percent frequently quoted. Of the ten fastest growing occupations cited by the Department of Labor in their ten-year projection, seven are in the computer and computer-related fields, with projections of some 1.5 million jobs in computers and electronics. The news is especially optimistic for women and minorities, who have in the past occupied less than 14 percent of the labor force. The latest prospects tend to indicate that women and minorities may comprise as much as 58 percent of the work force in the Labor Department's listing of Key Industries.

THE JOB SEARCH

Job hunting can be either a rewarding experience or one marked by frustration and disappointment. It's not enough to be technically qualified. You must research sources of employment, and more importantly, learn how to sell yourself to a prospective employer. Let's look first at how you find out who is hiring computer maintenance specialists. Once we have identified those companies and individuals responsible for hiring, we will examine and formulate a plan of action. That plan of action includes preparing a "sales brochure" on and about yourself—commonly called a résumé—making an initial contact, obtaining an interview, following up, and getting hired. We will also include a list of professional associations whose assistance can be invaluable to your job search and your professional development once you've joined the work force.

During the final stages of writing this book, I opened our regional newspaper and noted the following:

Electronics Technician

You will perform module and component-level remedial and preventive maintenance on microprocessor-based display terminals and personal computers.

To qualify, you will need experience in analog and digital theory, and working knowledge of XENIX and networking in a field service environment. Good written and verbal communications skills are necessary. An AA in Electronics is preferred.

Our company offers an excellent compensation and benefits package including the use of a company automobile. For immediate consideration, please send your résumé and salary history to us at . . . .

This is an actual ad that appeared in a Sunday edition of the *Atlanta Journal;* only the company's name and address have been deleted. Obviously, the local and regional newspaper classified sections are a good place to start—if you know what you're looking for and where to find it. If you haven't already guessed from the ad, not everyone calls a computer maintenance specialist by that name. Employment opportunities can be and are listed under a variety of titles. Some are logical, but others leave a great deal to the imagination, both from a prospective employee's point-of-view and in terms of the real needs of the employer.

The U.S. government publishes a comprehensive list of careers. This book is called the *Dictionary of Occupational Titles* and can be found in the reference section of larger libraries. All occupational categories are assigned a number code, which is of use to the prospective employee, employer, and the government's statisticians. Your guidance counselor may have a copy of this book or an abbreviated version of it on his or her bookshelf. For some reason, no specific DOT (dictionary of occupational title) code number has been assigned to cover computer service/engineering technicians. However, the following job classifications and DOT codes may be of use for a job search, especially if you avail yourself of your local state employment service:

Job Classification/Title	DOT Number
Test technician	019.161-014
Electronics assembler, developmental	726.261-010
Electronic sales and service technician	828.251-010
Electronics mechanic	828.281-010
Electronics mechanic apprentice	828.281-014
Mechanical test technician	869.261-014
Electromechanical technician	710.281-018

Keeping in mind that industry and the educational community don't always call something by a name that really describes it, let's examine some additional possible job titles that in fact still describe that career field you've just invested several years and several thousand dollars getting ready for:

- Field service engineer
- Data processing equipment mechanic
- Data processing equipment repair specialist
- Data systems installer
- Data systems technician
- Data processing configuration specialist
- Customer support engineer
- Customer service engineer
- Service engineer
- Computer mechanic
- Computer service technician
- Computer service specialist
- Computer repair person
- Medical electronics service engineer
- CAT field service engineer
- Biomedical engineering technologist (BMET)
- Clinical engineering specialist/technician

The list could go on for more pages than you'd like to read, or we'd like to write. There is a lack of a common and universal term to describe a person who is engaged in the profession of repairing and maintaining computers and computer systems. This lack of a common, acceptable title can make job searches interesting, to say the very least. But looking at this list or bemoaning the lack of a unified title isn't going to find you a job, so let's get back on course and begin a typical job search.

INFORMATION ABOUT EMPLOYERS

There are a number of ways to identify prospective employers and to alert them to your interest and availability for employment. The most obvious method has already been illustrated by the advertisement reprinted from a newspaper. The classified or want-ad sections of your local and regional newspapers carry requests from employers seeking qualified applicants for positions with their firms. In addition to your local newspapers, magazines and trade journals often carry help-wanted advertisements directed specifically to their readership.

A complete listing of publications of interest to computer professionals can be found in Appendix C of this book. Many of the magazines can be found at larger libraries or on newsstands. Advertisements in magazines or the newspapers are usually quite specific in their requirements and will invite you to write or call for more information. When an ad says write, it usually means to send in a copy of your résumé. Some of these ads will actually carry the name and address of the prospective employer. Others direct your response to a box number, usually in care of the publication. The former are called direct ads—that is, the employer openly identifies itself and invites a direct response. The latter form of ad, using a box number, is commonly referred to as a blind ad and is used by companies that wish to recruit personnel selectively and not be subjected to a deluge of job applicants arriving at their personnel office's door.

For the person who desires a career in the computer field, a very useful book is *Peterson's Guide to Engineering, Science, and Computer Jobs.* Published yearly, this book lists employers in the field who hire computer specialists for positions in service, research and development, information systems, production, technical service marketing, sales, and other areas. A brief description of each firm is included, basic information as to its specific hiring policy, starting salaries, and the name and address of the individual to whom your résumé must be sent. Additionally, Appendix B of this book contains a listing of many of the computer manufacturers as well as the names and addresses of third-party service organizations, all of whom hire and make use of the talents of computer maintenance specialists.

On a more direct and personal level, your college might sponsor what are commonly called job fairs. These are scheduled events that bring together hiring representatives from industry and students scheduled to graduate. The employer's representatives are there not only to screen prospective employees but to present information about their companies. It's a two-way selling opportunity. They are trying to sell you on their company. You are trying to sell them on you as an employee. Job fairs are also sponsored by organizations other than educational institutions. Your local employment service run by your state frequently holds these fairs to help prospective employees and employers get together. Other job fairs may be sponsored by private employment services that are retained by the clients to find suitable candidates to fill existing positions. In most cases, all of these events are designed to bring the two interested parties together. Interviews take place, and more often than not, job offers result.

Making the Most Important Sale of Your Life!

Armed with either a list of employers, ads from a newspaper, or an invitation to a job fair, you still lack one critical and necessary ingredient. This vital, make or break item is your "sales-brochure" or résumé. Without this piece of paper prospective employers have no way of quickly evaluating who you are and what you have done and are unable to make a value judgment as to your potential worth to their organization.

A résumé is not a chronological history of you, your family, and your experiences and personal habits. Many people have incorrectly perceived the résumé as a form of historical document that should list everything from your kindergarten teacher's name to how you spend your leisure time. Rather it is a concise presentation of you, your background, and experiences. It is the first crucial step in the process of selling yourself to a prospective employer.

THE RÉSUMÉ

A good résumé, like a newspaper article, deals with five key elements:

- Who
- What
- Why
- When
- How

Let's examine these elements in the context of a résumé and actually develop a usable product.

1. **Who.** This is the first key element of any résumé. It tells the employer who you are, where you live, and how to get in touch with you. In some cases, otherwise technically qualified applicants fail to hear from a company because their résumé lacks a current address and telephone number.
2. **What.** This is the purpose or objective of the résumé. If you are applying for a job, say so. If you know the job's title, this is the place to put it.
3. **Why.** Give the recruiter a reason or reasons why you are best suited for the position. Your education and any practical or work experience belong here. If you are uniquely qualified, say so, but be prepared to back up statements you make here at your interview.
4. **When.** The chronological summary of your education and work experiences in detail fits here. If you graduated with honors, say so. If you supported yourself by working part-time, resulting in somewhat longer of an educational time frame, say so. If you were trained on specific equipment, in-school, in the service, or on-the-job, or if you participated in special studies, say so!
5. **How.** Give recruiters something to remember you by. Tell them how you would be of assistance and value to their company. Be memorable, even in writing. Say something that sets you apart from the hundreds of others applying for the same job.

Writing Your Résumé

Before you can get hired you need a résumé. The résumé can get you an appointment and an interview. An interview can get you a job. Based on the five key elements and this schedule of events, let's create your résumé.

Before you begin writing, you will need to assemble some facts.

- Dates and locations of all educational training after elementary school.
- Dates, company names, and job descriptions of all positions you held during or after high school.
- A list containing the names, addresses, and telephone numbers of at least three people who know you and can be called upon to act as references.
- Additionally, you may want to assemble copies of high school diplomas and other educational certificates you may have already acquired. Transcripts from your last school together with any diploma or certificate should also be available.
- If available, an advertisement listing the positions you seek.

Once you have access to this information, you are ready to begin writing your résumé. There are certain established rules you should follow.

1. The résumé must be typewritten on white, business-sized (8 1/2″ × 11″) paper using a normal typeface. Under no circumstances should you use an italic or cursive typeface. You are writing a business document.
2. Use only one side of the paper and leave generous margins on both sides of the text and at the top and bottom. Try to confine your résumé to a single sheet. Statistics have proved that rarely is anyone hired from a résumé. It is merely a tool to present or sell yourself to the recruiter or personnel director.
3. Proofread your résumé carefully. It is best to let someone else reread the résumé once you are done to check for errors, poor grammar, and other problems. The final résumé should be typed free of errors. Avoid the use of correction fluid or correction tape.

Remember, the résumé is your primary sales tool. Its total objective is to get you an interview.

4. Do not include your date of birth, physical characteristics, marital status, or race. This information is neither required nor sought on a résumé. In fact, inclusion of this information, because of legislation and discrimination suits, may result in your résumé being ignored or discounted. Furthermore, under no circumstances include a photograph.

5. Write your résumé in the active tense. Be positive about yourself and your accomplishments and objectives. Once you have completed your résumé, you may wish to have it reproduced. Though photocopies are acceptable, using a local instant-printing service or a laser printer will result in a more professional appearance.

A Sample Résumé

The following is a fictitious but viable example of what a résumé for an entry-level position might look like. The subject has recently graduated from junior college and has a brief employment history.

JANE E. SAMUELS
8345 S. Adams Avenue
Sunnyland, GA 31001
(912) 555-9876

OBJECTIVE:	Entry-level position in computer maintenance where my education and skills can best be utilized.
EDUCATION:	Sunnyland Junior College, Sunnyland, Georgia, A.A.S. Program in Computer Technology and Electronics Engineering. Graduated with Honors, January 1993.
	Flint Senior High School, Sunnyland, Georgia, College-Preparatory Honors Program. Graduated June 1991.

| EMPLOYMENT | ComputerWorld, Sunnyland, Georgia. |
| January 1991–Present | *Service & Configuration Technician* |

Began part-time during school as technician-trainee; trained to deliver, install, and assist customers in the operation of small business computers and peripheral equipment. Performed routine maintenance on customers' equipment in shop and at customers' place of business. Employed on full-time basis since graduation from junior college.

Excellent References Furnished on Request

The Next Step

Now that you have a résumé, the next logical step is to use it to present yourself to prospective employers. This can be accomplished by written responses to advertisements, by physically handing the résumé to recruiters at job fairs, or by mailings to lists of employers. If you are mailing a résumé, either in response to an ad or as part of a mass mailing, you should prepare a brief cover letter stating the reason for your submission. This should be a brief statement or two about why you think you'd make a good employee and should invite the recipient to call you for an interview. Remember to include your name, address, and phone number. Without them, an excellent résumé and terrific cover letter won't accomplish their objective—getting you the interview.

THE INTERVIEW

You've done your homework, sent out letters and résumés, and your mailbox contains that all-important response, a request for an interview. No doubt it will be scheduled sometime in the future. You might even have to call to confirm the time, but the most important thing is that you've got your first interview! Now what do you do?

You prepared yourself before you wrote your résumé. A similar preparation is required for a successful interview. Some of the things personnel experts suggest include the following:

1. Try to find something out about your prospective employer. Your local library or perhaps friends working for the company can help.

2. Select the clothes you will wear in advance. Appearance is all important. You should be well groomed and neatly dressed in attire appropriate for a business environment. Too-casual, unclean, or unpressed clothes are out. Simple, tasteful suits and dresses are acceptable. For men, a trim haircut is a plus; for women, avoid excessive jewelry or strong perfume. For both, avoid any attire that will detract from the matter at hand, selling that company the best-qualified person—*you!*

3. Be sure to have a pen, list of references, and a copy of your résumé handy. You will probably have to fill out a formal application, so arrive a bit early.

4. Be polite, businesslike, and attentive. If you can project enthusiasm, you are establishing a positive image. Be prepared for questions from your interviewer, and likewise, have some questions of your own ready. Be prepared to take a technical qualification test. Many companies use this as a means of determining your skill level and how much you really know.

5. When you are asked questions, be concise and honest, and above all, be prepared. It's the unknown that frightens people. You might want to practice with a friend or relative to be sure that you will be able to handle yourself with poise and appear comfortable, even under stress.

6. Don't feel obligated to answer questions dealing with race, creed, national origin, marital status, or age. Questions of this sort are prohibited by law. A typical and acceptable response to this sort of questioning might be, "I'm not certain that these questions have any bearing on the position I'm applying for or my ability to do the job."

7. Remember, the interview process is a two-way street and a sales negotiation. You are selling yourself to the company; they in turn are buying, and they wish to acquire the best possible product.

8. Be sure to thank your interviewer and any other people you meet. Get their names and their business cards. Many successful job seekers follow up an interview with a brief thank you note reminding the person of your meeting, expressing your appreciation for the courtesy shown you, and "reminding" them of your interest in the job. Believe me, I've used it and it works!

If you've prepared properly, handled the questions well and with poise, and impressed everyone at the company, don't be surprised if the final words you hear are, "When can you start?" If that's the final word, then all that's left is a bit of negotiation about salary and the need to fill out insurance forms. You're on your way—congratulations. If you don't get an offer or they tell you they are still interviewing, don't despair. I had a job offer nearly a year after the initial interview. Keep trying. Practice makes perfect.

PROFESSIONAL ASSOCIATIONS

The following list of associations is comprised of organizations of interest to people either employed in the computer field or seeking employment. This is a partial list and does not reflect all of the many organizations that are now interested or involved in the high-technology field. We suggest you write directly to those organizations of interest to you for more information and membership requirements. Frequently these groups offer job placement assistance services to their membership.

American Federation of Information Processing Societies, Inc.
1815 North Lynn Street
Arlington, VA 22209

American Society for Information Science
1010 Sixteenth Street, NW
Washington, DC 20036

Association for Computing Machinery
11 West Forty-second Street
New York, NY 10036

Association for Educational Data Systems
1201 Sixteenth Street, NW
Washington, DC 20036

IEEE Computer Society
  1109 Spring Street
  Silver Spring, MD 20910

      or

  10622 Los Vaqueros Circle
  Los Alamitos, CA 90720

Instrument Society of America
  Box 12277
  Research Triangle Park, NC 27709

American Association for Medical Systems & Information
  4405 East-West Highway
  Bethesda, MD 20814

Association for Women in Computing
  407 Hillmoor Drive
  Silver Spring, MD 20901

Computer and Business Equipment Manufacturers Association
  311 First Street, NW
  Washington, DC 20001

CHAPTER 9

EMPLOYMENT OUTLOOK

The last chapter covered some of the methods you use to find out about employers and to prepare for and get a job interview. Although there may be some who read the information, follow the suggestions, and do actually get their first interview and job, there will be a lot of people who do not. Finding the job that's right for you takes time and may require you to make decisions that could mean changing your place of residence, life-style, or other parts of your personal life.

Computer maintenance and high technology in general is a field that all experts agree will consistently have more job opportunities than applicants for at least the foreseeable future. However, many of these opportunities will not be found in your local community. Some may require relocation, others both relocation and extensive travel.

INDEPENDENT CONTRACTING

Another, somewhat unique, opportunity requires relocation, travel, and short- and long-term assignments. Many individuals and companies have opted to hire technical personnel as independent contractors. These people are usually experienced in a given field and become temporary members of a company for the duration of a specific project. Independent contractors are essentially self-employed business professionals who hire themselves out to a company under a contract for a specific project and/or time period. Unlike regular employees, contractors do not receive regular employee benefits. They are paid only when they work, must pay their own medical insurance premiums, and are responsible for all tax liabilities.

On the plus side, their salaries are far and above those normally paid to a "captive-employee"—that is, a regularly employed member of a given company. Computer service specialists and other members of the high-technology field are especially suited and welcomed by these companies. For example, according to our salary survey found in Appendix A, a technical writer or editor with one or two years of experience would earn an average of $24,630. The same individual working as an independent contractor would receive an average salary of $25 per hour or $52,000 for the same year's work. Computer maintenance specialists with two or more years of experience could earn as much as $21 per hour, or $43,680 per year.

Although the salaries are obviously higher, you must take some facts into consideration:

1. You are personally responsible for filing your state and federal income taxes and ensuring that you have made sufficient estimates and deposits to cover your tax liabilities as well as making contributions to social security.
2. You must obtain and pay the full cost of health care insurance and life insurance as well as optional disability insurance.
3. You must be flexible enough to take one assignment in California, and when it ends be ready to move on to Maine. You also must be able to function well with many different people and be extremely confident and competent in your specific area of expertise. Likewise, you have to be prepared to endure periods of unemployment between assignments.
4. On the positive side, you are a self-employed businessperson entitled to many tax advantages you would not normally have as a regular employee at a company. Your travel expenses and living expenses at motels and hotels are all deductible from your income subject to certain guidelines and limitations, and you have a unique opportunity to grow in your field by gaining experience from each and every project you participate in.

5. You are to a great extent in total control of your destiny. Tax laws permit you to establish excellent retirement programs that are more complete than those usually associated with a permanent position. Your schedule can be as flexible as you wish. Wintering in warm climates and spending summers in cooler areas of the country are possible along with the ability to work for as long a period during the year as you deem necessary.

6. All of this might sound inviting, but you should keep in mind that you are a temporary contractor at a given company. Your services are being used for a specific project and specific time period. If you desire security and retirement after twenty years with one company, this isn't the way for you to go. If this does seem interesting to you, the address for *C. E. Weekly,* the digest for contract employees, can be found in Appendix C. Additionally, the same source has an informative videotape that explains how to become a high-tech contractor and includes the advantages and disadvantages of this form of work.

WORK WHEREVER YOU WANT

No matter what path you elect to take, either as a contract or permanent employee, the rapid growth of the computer maintenance field has made opportunities available in all areas of the country. No longer must you restrict your job search to a specific city, town, or state. As a skilled high-technology specialist, you can locate yourself and your skills in virtually any part of the United States and in many foreign countries. The salary survey provided in Appendix A takes into account eight geographical settings in the continental United States:

- *New England:* Connecticut, New Hampshire, and Massachusetts.
- *Middle Atlantic:* Maryland, New York, New Jersey, Pennsylvania, and Washington, D.C.
- *East North Central:* Ohio, Michigan, Indiana, Kentucky, and northern New York (Buffalo, Rochester, and Albany)

- *West North Central:* Missouri, Illinois, Wisconsin, Nebraska, and Minnesota
- *South Atlantic:* Georgia, North Carolina, South Carolina, and Florida
- *South Central:* Texas, Tennessee, Arkansas, Louisiana, and Oklahoma
- *Mountain:* New Mexico, Colorado, Arizona, and Utah
- *Pacific:* California, Washington, and Oregon

Think Carefully Before You Say No

It's quite obvious that the entire United States is open to your employment search. Naturally, there are some regions where you may not want to live. These regions usually have high costs-of-living or other such problems. However, in many of the more expensive parts of the country salaries are correspondingly higher to take into account housing costs and other intangibles. Never reject an offer out-of-hand merely because the position is located in what you perceive to be an expensive area to live. There are usually trade-offs. The south-central region isn't known for excessively high salaries, at least on the entry level, but this is mitigated by a more moderate climate and generally lower housing costs. So before you say no, study all of the alternatives. If you enjoy skiing and it's an important part of your life off the job, then an assignment to southern Florida will not make you as happy as one in Colorado, unless, of course, you can water-ski.

Evaluate a company based on what it has to offer, not just immediately, but in the future. Ask yourself where you might be three, five, or ten years from now. Is there room for advancement within the company, or do promotions come from outside? Are the coworkers you've met the sort of people you'd pick as friends? Is the plant's location in an area you feel comfortable with, not just for yourself, but for raising children in the future? Salary may just not be everything; look around you and be sure this is what you want. Check the company's history, progress, and place in the market. This information will probably be given to you at an interview in the form of an annual report. Remember, your first job should be chosen as carefully as your last. If all conditions are right, it may just be the job you will still hold twenty years from now.

JOBS AND JOB DESCRIPTIONS

We have discussed the fact that there is no single acceptable job title to cover the career of computer maintenance, and that may, without our list, make a job search a bit harder. You should, when looking through the classified ads, check these sections:

- Computers
- Data Processing
- Electronics
- Engineering
- Management
- Marketing
- Medical (for Biomedical Tech/Clinical Tech)
- Sales
- Service
- Skilled Trades
- Technical

These headings should contain the sorts of jobs you'd be interested in. They will give you a title, a brief line or two about the position, and how to apply. But how can you tell much about the job and its requirements from one of those 30-line, 3-day, $30 ads? Try examining these representative job descriptions obtained from some companies that actually hire computer maintenance personnel:

Representative Job Descriptions

FIELD SERVICE REPRESENTATIVE MEDICAL ELECTRONICS

Education:

1. *Junior field service representative.* High school graduate plus one to two years college-level electronics technology training or equivalent. Up to two years of practical experience in electronic maintenance, especially in computers and digital circuitry.
2. *Associate field service representative.* Same as above except for one to three years experience in electronic maintenance of medically related equipment.

3. *Field service representative.* Same as above except for three to six years of experience in electronic maintenance of medically related equipment.
4. *Senior field service representative.* Same as above except requires more than five years of experience in maintenance of medically related electronics.

Primary Job Function:

To provide various types of technical and ancillary services to customers of our Patient Monitoring and Electronic Flow Control Systems to ensure customer satisfaction with the equipment, its performance, installation, and regulatory requirements with a minimum of supervision.

Tasks and/or Duties.

1. Preinstallation planning in coordination with sales personnel and customers to ensure efficient and satisfactory equipment/system installations.
2. Installation of equipment/systems in accordance with customer's requirements and the requirements of regulatory agencies.
3. Troubleshooting and the repair or replacement of existing equipment in a judicious manner.
4. Preventive maintenance inspections of existing equipment.
5. Coordination with hospital operational biomedical and maintenance personnel regarding in-warranty equipment problems.
6. Coordination with the cognizant hospital personnel regarding preventive maintenance inspections under service contracts.
7. Public relations visits with purchasing and other administrative hospital personnel.
8. The sales of service contracts and accessory items.
9. In-service to operational and technical personnel to ensure maximum utilization of the equipment.
10. Spare equipment depot and replacement parts management to maintain an optimum level of spare items.
11. Coordination with local sales personnel regarding customer's problems, the customer's attitudes, and potential new business opportunities.

12. Coordination with the field service manager and the main service department on a regular basis as well as normal required reporting procedures.
13. Manage day-to-day overtime and operational costs to minimize total field service operational costs.
14. Always present a professional manner to customers, sales personnel, and corporate representatives.

Physical and Mental Environment:

Mental: Troubleshooting and analysis require concentration and ability to trace problems through a decision path. Pressure exerted by customers requires maintaining a positive professional attitude.

Physical: Includes lifting, loading, and unloading equipment weighing up to sixty pounds.

Environment: Must be able to work in areas from sterile conditions to construction sites.

Salary Range[1]:

1. Junior field representative—$18,200 per year.
2. Associate field representative—$22,500 per year.
3. Field service representative—$31,250 per year.
4. Senior field service representative—$38,500 per year.

COMPUTER MAINTENANCE TECHNICIANS, FACTORY/DEPOT REPAIR

Education:

1. *Associate electronic technician.* ASEE program and/or some combination of work and educational experience in the component level repair of computer systems and peripherals at the field and/or depot site. Working knowledge of electronics test equipment as well as excellent verbal and written skills required.

---

[1] The salary figures are based on an hourly rate with overtime paid, and do not include commissions earned for selling contracts, supplies, or the use of a company supplied car. The actual average compensation value for a starting associate field service representative is closer to $32,850 per year when these various incentives are taken into consideration.

2. *Electronics Technician.* Same as above plus two to four years of experience in system repairs.
3. *Senior Electronics Technician.* Same as above plus minimum of four to six years experience and ability to interface with and provide technical supervision to fellow employees in a professional business environment.

Primary Job Functions:

Provide high-quality, cost-effective repairs of products and modules to provide for an effective utilization of the Field Service inventory and provide timely turnaround of customer products and to enhance the quality image of the company's products.

Tasks and/or Duties.

1. Associate electronics technician. Working under the technical supervision of a senior product specialist:
   a. Perform repair of defective modules to the component level.
   b. Perform repair of defective product returned by ISD customers.
   c. Perform unit level repair and refurbishment of new and used computer and peripheral equipment as required.
   d. Perform logic board rework as required.
   e. Perform other duties as assigned.
2. Electronics technician. With minimum supervision perform the following:
   a. Perform repair of defective modules to the component level. Perform quality assurance testing on completed repairs.
   b. Perform repair of defective products returned by ISD customers. Perform quality assurance testing on completed repairs.
   c. Provide technical assistance to external repair vendors, distributors, dealers, and users by telephone. May travel as required.
   d. Perform unit level repair and refurbishment of new and used computer and peripheral equipment as required.
   e. Perform other duties as assigned.
3. Senior electronics technician. With no supervision perform the following:
   a. Perform repair of defective modules to the component level. Perform quality assurance testing on completed repairs.

    b. Perform repair of defective products returned by ISD customers. Perform quality assurance testing on completed repairs.

    c. Perform quality assurance testing on repairs made by associate electronics technician and the electronic technician as well as provide supervision and direction to them both.

    d. Provide technical assistance to external repair vendors, distributors, dealers, and users by telephone. May be required to travel.

    e. Provide task scheduling subject to shop load as defined by department management.

Salary Range:

1. Associate electronics technician: from $18,275 to $28,080 per year.
2. Electronics technician: from $21,225 to $31,200 per year.
3. Senior electronics technician: from $32,150 to $44,650 per year.

EMPLOYMENT SUMMARY

Regardless of what approach you take, be assured that you won't be expected to know everything about the company's equipment. You will be given the opportunity to participate in a variety of educational experiences, including specific training on the company's products as well as continuing education to make you more valuable to your company and at the same time to put you in a position to earn more.

Remember as you prepare for the challenges of tomorrow and the tomorrows to come: Nothing is impossible if you really apply yourself and have a good educational foundation and positive attitude. The future belongs to you!

SALARY SURVEY

This salary survey reflects data collected from a total of eight geographical divisions of the United States: New England, Mid-Atlantic, East North Central, West North Central, South Atlantic, South Central, Mountain, and Pacific. It represents the high, low, and average salaries reported for the computer-related positions discussed in Chapter 2.

Job Title	High	Low	Average
(salaries are given in thousands of dollars)			
Computer service specialist			
Entry Level	24.5	17.1	20.8
1–2 years	33	26	29.5
2–5 years	43	36.5	39.75
5 years +	51.5	40.1	45.8
PC/microprocessor analyst			
1–2 years	37.25	25.25	31.25
2–5 years	40.5	30.1	35.3
5 years +	51.7	35.8	43.75
Systems software programmer			
1–2 years	33.7	26.8	30.25
2–5 years	38.1	32.46	35.28
5 years +	47.8	35.9	41.85
Communications/tech specialists			
1–2 years	33.9	18.10	26.0
2–5 years	42.25	24.1	33.17
5 years +	49.1	30.5	39.8

Job Title	High	Low	Average
	(salaries are given in thousands of dollars)		
Technical writer/editor			
1–2 years	29.5	19.75	24.63
2–5 years	36.9	27.75	32.33
5 years +	40.2	29.5	34.9
Senior analyst/lead/consultant			
2–5 years	41.9	31.0	27.77
5–7 years	47.6	34.0	41.7
Technical service manager			
Small	46.5	35.4	40.9
Medium	58.5	40.75	49.63
Large	67.6	44.75	56.18
Sales (Capital Eq.)			
Hardware	59.75	46.75	53.25
Services	58.8	35.0	46.9
Software	59.4	39.8	49.6
Sales Managers	75.6	50.0	62.8

Note: These figures were derived from a variety of sources including private employment counselors, Department of Labor statistics, private industry sources, and other contributors.

APPENDIX B

CORPORATE AND
INDUSTRIAL EMPLOYERS

PC DESKTOP COMPUTER MANUFACTURERS

Acer Technologies Corp.
    401 Charcot Avenue
    San Jose, CA 95131

Advanced Logic Research Inc.
    10 Chrysler Avenue
    Irvine, CA 92718

Alpha Omega Computer Products
    18612 Ventura Boulevard
    Tarzana, CA 91356

Alphanumeric International
    13360 E. Firestone Boulevard
    Suite F
    Santa Fe Springs, CA 90670

American Computer & Peripherals Inc.
    2720 Croddy Way
    Santa Ana, CA 92704

American Micro Technology
    14751 Ben Franklin Avenue
    Tustin, CA 92680

AMQ Computer Corp.
    1901 Bascom Avenue, #340
    Campbell, CA 95008

Apparat Inc.
    6801 S. Dayton Street
    Englewood, CO 80112

Apple Computer Inc.
    20525 Mariani Avenue
    Cupertino, CA 95014

AST Research Inc.
    2121 Alton Avenue
    Irvine, CA 92714

AT&T Information Systems
    One Speedwell Avenue
    Morristown, NJ 07960

Beltron Computers
    10501 Decatur Road
    Philadelphia, PA 19154

Bentley Computers
    1700 Still Meadow Cove
    Round Rock, TX 78681

Bi-Tech Enterprises
    10 Carlough Road
    Bohemia, NY 11716

Bondwell
    47358 Fremount Boulevard
    Fremount, CA 94538

CAD Counsel
    5032 Lankershim Boulevard
    North Hollywood, CA 91601

Canon USA Inc.
    One Canon Plaza
    Lake Success, NY 11042

Chicago Computer Connection
    5239 N. Harlem Avenue
    Chicago, IL 60656

Club American Technologies
    3401 W. Warren Avenue
    Fremont, CA 95439

Compaq Computer Corp.
    20555 FM 149
    Houston, TX 77070

Computerland
30985 Santana Street
Hayward, CA 94544

Data General Corp.
4400 Computer Drive
Westboro, MA 01580

Electro-Design Inc.
690 Rancheros Drive
San Marcos, CA 92069

Eltech Research Inc.
1725 McCandless
Milpitas, CA 95035

Epson America Inc.
2780 Lomita Boulevard
Torrance, CA 90505

Five Star Computers
3220 Commander Drive
Dallas, TX 75006

Franklin Telecommunications
733 Lakefield Road
West Lake Village, CA 91361

Generic Technologies Inc.
9812 Pfiumm Road
Lenexa, KS 66215

Gulfstream Micro Systems
1065 S. Rogers Circle
Boca Raton, FL 33487

Heath Company
Post Office Box 1288
Benton Harbor, MI 49022

IBM
100 Summit Avenue
Montvale, NJ 07645

Indtech Corp.
1275 Hammerwood Avenue
Sunnyvale, CA 94089

Intelligent Micro Systems
1633 Babcock, Suite 424
San Antonio, TX 78229

JC Information Systems
  161 Whitney Place
  Fremont, CA 94539

Leading Edge Products Inc.
  225 Turnpike Street
  Canton, MA 02021

Manufacturers Design Source
  620 W. Center
  North Salt Lake, UT 84054

Micro Five Corp.
  3500 Hyland Avenue
  Costa Mesa, CA 92626

Mini-Micro Business Systems
  Post Office Box 13063
  Boulder, CO 80308

Mitsubishi Electronics America Inc.
  Computer Systems Division
  991 Knox Street
  Torrance, CA 90502

NCR Corp.
  1700 S. Patterson Boulevard
  Dayton, OH 45479

Olivetti USA
  Office Products Division
  765 US Highway 202
  Somerville, NJ 08876

PC Designs Inc.
  2500 N. Hemlock Circle
  Broken Arrow, OK 74012

PC Discount Inc.
  2758 Bingle Road
  Houston, TX 77055

PC Source
  12303-G Technology Boulevard
  Austin, TX 78727

PC's Limited Inc.
  1611 Headway Circle Bldg. 3
  Austin, TX 78754

Prism MicroSystems
  18226 W. McDurmott
  Irvine, CA 92714

Proteus Technology Corp.
  377 Route 17
  Airport # 17 Center
  Hasbruck Heights, NJ 07604

Sanyo Business Systems
  51 Joseph Street
  Monnachie, NJ 07074

SCSI
  10525 Hombolt Street
  Los Alamitos, CA 90720

Tandon Corp.
  405 Science Drive
  Moorpark, CA 93021

Tandy Corp.
  Radio Shack Computer
  Merchandising
  One Tandy Center
  Fort Worth, TX 76102

Tatung of America
  2850 El Presido Street
  Long Beach, CA 90810

Televideo Systems
  1170 Morse Avenue
  Sunnyvale, CA 94088

Telex Computer Products
  6422 E. Forty-first Street
  Tulsa, OK 74135

United Solutions Inc.
  1107 Main Street
  Georgetown, TX 78626

Victor Technologies Inc.
  380 El Pueblo Road
  Scotts Valley, CA 95066

Wang Laboratories Inc.
  1 Industrial Avenue
  Lowell, MA 01851

Wyse Technology
    3571 N. First Street
    San Jose, Ca 95134

XTRA Business Systems
    2350 Qume Drive
    San Jose, CA 95131

Zenith Data Systems
    1000 Milwaukee Avenue
    Glenview, IL 60025

MAINTENANCE SERVICE COMPANIES

3M Equipment Services & Supply Division
    Building 220-9W-07
    3M Center
    St. Paul, MN 55144

Bunker Ramo Corp.
    2 Enterprise Drive
    Shelton, CT 06484

Businessland
    10001 Ridder Park Drive
    San Jose, CA 95131

Carterfone Maintenance
    Services Division
    1341 W. Mockingbird Lane,
    Suite 1100
    Dallas, TX 75247

Computer Maintenance Corp.
    405 Murray Hill Parkway
    East Rutherford, NJ 07073

Control Data Corp.
    1101 E. Seventy-eighth Street
    Bloomington, MN 55420

Data Link Inc.
    608 Washington Avenue
    Bridgeville, PA 15017

Decision Data Service Inc.
    1 Progress Avenue
    Horsham, PA 19044

Eastern Business Machines Inc.
  Capital Office Park
  6303 Ivy Lane
  Greenbelt, MD 20770

Electro Rent Corp.
  4209 Vanowen Place
  Burbank, CA 91505

GE Computer Service
  2885 Pacific Drive
  Norcross, GA 30071

Harris Corp.
  11262 Indian Trail
  Dallas, TX 75229

Honeywell Bull Inc.
  Customer Service Division
  165 Needham Street
  Newton Highlands, MA 02161

ICON Computer Corp.
  1232 A.S. Village Way
  Santa Ana, CA 92705

Integrated Automation
  1745 Tullie Circle, NE
  Atlanta, GA 30329

Lesametric Corp.
  Data Communications Division
  1164 Triton Drive
  Foster City, CA 94404

Momentum Service Corp.
  201 Littleton Road
  Morris Plains, NJ 07950

National Micro Rentals Inc.
  43 Stouts Lane
  South Brunswick, NJ 08852

NCR Corp., Customer Service Division
  9391 Washington Church Road
  Miamisburg, OH 45342

PC ServNet
  5655 Lindero Canyon Road
  Suite 221
  Westlake Village, CA 91362

Peripheral Maintenance Inc.
  16-6 Passaic Avenue
  Fairfield, NJ 07006

Personal Computer Services Inc.
  104 E. Twenty-third Street
  New York, NY 10010

Pritronix
  2629 N. Stemmons, Suite 200
  Dallas, TX 75207

RTK Communications Group
  Computer Services Division
  215 Wood Avenue
  Middlesex, NJ 08846

Servcom
  1515 W. Fourteenth Street
  Tempe, AZ 85281

Sorbus
  50 E. Swedesford Road
  Frazer, PA 19355

Terminals Unlimited Inc.
  360 S. Washington Street
  Falls Church, VA 22046

TRW Customer Service Division
  15 Law Drive
  Fairfield, NJ 07006

TSSI
  81 Croton Avenue
  Ossining, NY 10562

Unisys
  Post Office Box 500
  Blue Bell, PA 19424

Use-'R Computers Inc.
  5929 Baker Road, Suite 490
  Minnetonka, MN 55345

Western Union
  1 Lake Street
  Upper Saddle River, NJ 07458

WISCO Computer Services
 1600A Ellsworth Drive
 Industrial Drive, NW
 Atlanta, GA 30318

XEROX Corp.
 Xerox Square
 Rochester, NY 14644

PERIODICALS AND TRADE PUBLICATIONS

A+ (Apple users' magazine)
11 Davis Drive
Belmont, CA 94002

Business Computer Systems
221 Columbus Avenue
Boston, MA 02116

Byte
70 Main Street
Peterborough, NH 03458

C. E. Weekly
Post Office Box 97000
Kirkland, WA 98083-9700

Classroom Computer News
51 Spring Street
Watertown, MA 02172

Computer (IEEE Computer Society)
10622 Los Vaqueros Circle
Los Alamitos, CA 90720

Computer Dealer
20 Community Place
Morristown, NJ 07960

Computer Decisions
50 Essex Street
Rochelle Park, NJ 07662

Computer Design
11 Goldsmith Street
Littleton, MA 01406

Computer & Electronics Marketing
   820 Second Avenue
   New York, NY 10017

Computer/Electronic Service News
   CESN Publications Inc.
   20 Grove Street
   Peterborough, NH 03458

Computer Retail News
   600 Community Drive
   Manhasset, NY 11030

Computer Shopper
   Post Office Box 1419
   Titusville, FL 32781-9988

Computer Systems News
   600 Community Drive
   Manhasset, NY 11030

Computerworld
   Post Office Box 880
   Framingham, MA 01701

Datamation
   875 Third Avenue
   New York, NY 10022

Desktop Publishing
   Suite 180
   2055 Woodside Road
   Redwood City, CA 94061

Digital Design
   1050 Commonwealth Avenue
   Boston, MA 02215

ECN (Electronic Component News)
   Chilton Way
   Radnor, PA 19089

EDN (Electronic Design News)
   221 Columbus Avenue
   Boston, MA 02116

Electronic Business
   221 Columbus Avenue
   Boston, MA 02116

Electronic Engineering Times
  600 Community Drive
  Manhasset, NY 11030

Electronic News
  7 E. Twelfth Street
  New York, NY 10003

Field Service Manager
  Association of Field Service
    Managers International
  6361 Presidential Court
  Suite B
  Fort Myers, FL 33919

Government Data Systems
  475 Park Avenue South
  New York, NY 10016

High Technology
  38 Commercial Warf
  Boston, MA 02110

Information Week
  600 Community Drive
  Manhassett, NY 11030

InfoWorld
  1060 Marsh Road
  Menlo Park, CA 94025

Interface Age
  16704 Marquardt Avenue
  Cerritos, CA 90701

Medical Electronics
  2994 W. Liberty Avenue
  Pittsburgh, PA 15216

MIS Week
  7 E. Twelfth Street
  New York, NY 10003

PC Magazine
  One Park Avenue
  New York, NY 10016

PC Resources
  80 Elm Street
  Peterborough, NH 03458

PC Tech Journal
    One Park Avenue
    New York, NY 10016

PC Week
    15 Crawford Street
    Needham, MA 02194

PC World
    555 DeHaro Street
    San Francisco, CA 94107

Personal Computing
    10 Mulholland Drive
    Hasbrouck Heights, NJ 07604

Radio Electronics
    500-B Bi-County Boulevard
    Farmingdale, NY 11735

The Electron
    Cleveland Institute of Electronics
    4781 E. 355th Street
    Willoughby, OH 44094